Writer. Producer. Engineer.

A Handbook for Creating Contemporary Commercial Music

by Michael Farquharson

Edited by Susan Gedutis Lindsay and Jonathan Feist
Contributing Editors: Jay Kennedy and Matthew Nicholl

Berklee Press

Vice President: David Kusek
Dean of Continuing Education: Debbie Cavalier
Managing Editor: Jonathan Feist
Director of Business Affairs: Robert F. Green
Senior Designer: Robert Heath

ISBN-13: 978-0-87639-053-5
ISBN-10: 0-87639-053-X

DISTRIBUTED BY

Berklee Press
1140 Boylston Street
Boston, MA 02215-3693 USA
617-747-2146
Visit Berklee Press Online at
berkleepress.com

HAL•LEONARD®
CORPORATION
7777 W. BLUEMOUND RD. P.O. BOX 13819
MILWAUKEE, WISCONSIN 53213
Visit Hal Leonard Online at
www.halleonard.com

This book is dedicated to my wonderful wife Aytul,

who was incredibly supportive throughout

the countless hours, weeks, and months

I spent at the computer, surrounded by

stacks of papers, notes, books, and documents.

She never stopped supporting

and encouraging me.

☙

Contents

Acknowledgments

Thanks to everyone at Berklee Media who made this book possible: with many special thanks and great appreciation to Susan Gedutis Lindsay and Jonathan Feist, for their tireless efforts, hard work, and support, and to Debbie Cavalier for giving me this great opportunity and believing in this book from the beginning. I also thank Dr. Jay Kennedy for going over the book with a fine-toothed comb to ensure its accuracy, and Matthew Nicholl, Chair of Contemporary Writing and Production at Berklee, for his support and final read-through.

This book would not have been possible without the many people in Toronto and Boston who gave me the opportunity to have a career in music that allowed me to learn and grow.

A special thanks to all of my great students over the years at Berklee College of Music and Humber College in Toronto, who inspired me in the first place.

Writer, Producer, and Engineer

WRITING CONTEMPORARY MUSIC has become a multidimensional process. That's a relatively recent change. Today's writers of commercial music must also produce and engineer their own projects.

Before the 1960s, these roles were usually distinct. Even singers and songwriters were different people. The Beatles and Bob Dylan helped bring forth a new era in which artists could be more autonomous in their creations. Technological advances in each decade since then have brought forth new levels of artistic self-sufficiency.

The business of using music encourages this one-stop shopping, as well. By using writers with capabilities to produce and engineer their own recordings, clients can get a better product faster and more cheaply than ever before. The industry strongly favors writers with multidimensional skills. Cutting studio costs out of the equation is a major cost savings. Once clients learned that they could get the same product for $5,000 that they had been getting for $10,000, the model of separate writer and studio no longer made business sense for many applications.

Now, we writers must wear three hats: one with a W (writer) on it, one with a P (producer), and one with an E (engineer). You need to be able to change hats on a dime. The roles are fully integrated, particularly those of writer/producer. In this book, I will try to give you insights into being successful at all three, as part of a single process based on a sound business strategy.

In essence, the roles are like this:

The **writer** is the creative artist. When you're wearing your W hat, you are conversant in all musical styles, and can compose a song, a symphony, or a soundtrack. You can close your eyes and imagine a melody that captures the essential emotional core of dog food or rising profits or an army of aliens. This book will discuss some of the creative parameters for different types of writing projects. Some books about the craft of writing music are listed in the Resources appendix.

The **producer** is the objective ear and controls the business aspect of your career. When you're wearing your P hat, you're ensuring that the clients are getting the music they need, and that your compensation is in order. The producer is the business head and the recording supervisor. You are the hub. Everything about the project ultimately answers to you.

The **engineer** renders the recording. When wearing your E hat, you're not listening to music as a creative entity of passion. You're listening to the sound and painting a picture. You're focused on revealing the composition in its best light and ensuring that the physical recording conforms to the client's technical requirements.

In a world where thousands of other writers are trying to do the same job you are, your success will depend in large part on the high caliber of the final product—both artistically and technically. To be a competitive music writer/producer, you need to know as much as possible about every aspect of the music writing and producing business, from outboard gear and digital recording to musical styles and recording studio etiquette—not to mention the ins and outs of composing and producing, copyright law, and accounting—all while remaining true to your artistic goals and maintaining focus on your music.

After working in the commercial music industry for many years, as a writer/producer/engineer and also as a bass player, I joined the Berklee faculty, to teach these skills. I have had the opportunity to help hundreds of students launch their careers.

In this book, I present some of their stories, some technical advice, and some strategic guidance, which I've seen lead to successful careers many times over. Many of my Berklee alumni are doing great things and enjoying terrific careers in this industry. I'll try to explain how they are doing it and why they are successful. I hope this makes your own journey easier, whether you are beginning a new career as a writer or are trying to expand your current writing business.

Enjoy. May your recordings sound breathtaking, and as a result, express your music in the way that you imagine it.

—*Michael Farquharson*

PART I

Business and Process

The first part of this book focuses on the business of being a writer/producer. We will look at the process of setting up your business, getting information about the industry, and processes of running the business, such as finding work, getting paid, and working with musicians.

CHAPTER **1**

Business Strategy for Writers

AS A WRITER, YOU CREATE THE MUSIC. As a producer, you oversee and generally participate in the entire creative and technical process, including any business aspects. Commercial writer/producers may write for film, video, television, advertising, Web sites, videogames, multimedia presentations, cellular phone ring tones, or any other context that may arise. Every project is unique and each will pose unique challenges. Occasionally, you may be asked to produce someone else's music.

It's a complex way to make a living, and it's essential that you have a strong grasp of the business considerations it requires.

There's the old joke: What question do you never want to ask, as a musician?

Answer: "Do you want fries with that?"

You will need to take care of business, if you are to have a fruitful career in this industry.

Teaching at Berklee and working in the commercial music field for so long have given me the opportunity to watch hundreds of writers piece their careers together. Many are surprised to find that the most successful graduates aren't necessarily the best writers or best musicians. Those who succeed are the most professional and the most strategic. Uncompromising "artistes" often find themselves working outside the field. But those who are organized and can consistently deliver a good product are the ones who make it.

In this book, I'll try to help you to understand and achieve the necessary standards, as a writer, and to build a strategy that's likely to lead you towards a successful career in writing music. These strategies will help you get more writing projects.

On the first day of my *Music Writing and Production* class, I write this on the whiteboard:

music BUSINESS

Get it? It's mostly about business. The music business works pretty much like any other business, and you need a business outlook to succeed. The music part will drive your passion, but you need to put a major effort on creating your business, just as you would any other entrepreneurial endeavor. Writers quickly learn that most of the workings of the music business are business based, not music based. Any commercial endeavor's survival depends on it being founded on strong business principles. A common weakness among musicians is the yearning to live in an ivory tower, focusing exclusively on creating art, and not enough on the bottom line. But to succeed, you need to understand business.

This means planning your business strategy carefully. You need a clear grasp of the type of work you want to do, how much money it will bring in, and what your expenses will be. Managing these effectively will give you the best chance of success. If you've been struggling, fine-tuning your strategy and focus may lead to the breakthrough you are seeking.

Creating a solid business strategy—even writing up a formal "business plan" document—is among your most important career steps as a music writer. In adhering to a well-considered strategy, you will focus on creating and managing the business that you want.

Your ultimate goal in this strategic plan is to articulate in as precise detail as possible how you will earn enough income to succeed. Without crafting this, your business is likely to fail. Developing a formal business plan will help you to focus and design a strategy that will work.

The physical plan itself could benefit by being many pages long, but as long as the essential balance of income and expenses are there, it will fulfill its primary function.

Though you are first and foremost an artist, recognize that this is not what will encourage people to put their money behind you. There are many other writers out there vying for the same jobs as you are. You need to assure your potential clients that you can do the job—that you can deliver good quality music on time.

COMPONENTS OF AN EFFECTIVE STRATEGY

Let's look at the necessary components that make for an effective business strategy.

1. SCHEDULE

Projecting a timeline of what happens at what point of your career will help you keep faith in difficult times. Think in terms of at least a year or two, not day to day.

Allow time for your business to grow and blossom. Many writers give up too soon. Paying your dues is a part of this business. This means time developing your craft, researching the business climate, and often taking low-paying jobs.

This time is a necessary career investment. Allow for it in your game plan. Have in your mind a certain amount of time that you'll invest into getting your career off the ground—an amount of time during which you won't give up.

Create a calendar/timeline, showing what you'll do in the near and long term, towards developing your career. This is important at all stages of your career.

Without a long-term view of time, beginning writers especially are likely to quit too soon. They find themselves saying, "I didn't go to school all those years to work for free, getting coffee for people. This sucks. I can't live like this."

But countless successful writers did get coffee. At the same time, they got to know people, and gained insight into how the industry worked. It was a necessary mountain to climb.

Similarly, established writers trying to get into new areas of writing—say, scoring films or TV shows—need to give efforts towards new directions time to take hold. Marketing needs time to find its audience, and networking takes time to bring the right people into your circle of contacts.

I recently got a call from a former student, who I'll call Sue. Sue was a good singer and writer, and a bit more mature than the average student—a couple years older. After she graduated, she got an internship in New York, working for free at a big jingle company. Others bailed, but she kept at it. For six months, she kept in her role, doing her job—but also writing and producing personal projects, on her own time. And then, finally, a job in business/promotion came up within that jingle house, and they hired her. Now, she'll get into the real business end of it, make more and better connections, and have a much easier time transitioning into a more creative position. She had a game plan; it was what she said she'd do all along, and it's working out great for her.

Sue's projected timeline might have looked like this:

May 2005	Graduate Berklee, move to NYC.
July 2005	Get any job at a big music production company in NYC, even an unpaid internship.
August 2005	Complete résumé and business cards as a writer. Have plan for researching the jingle industry in NYC. Have at least five new musician contacts and three leads on good studios.
September 2005	Get home studio fully operational. Have leads to at least two freelance writing/production projects. Understand microphone technique, and research what vocal microphone I should buy.
January 2006	Buy really great vocal microphone. Have at least twenty studio-musician contacts, with duplicates in all rhythm section instruments. Know at least two local freelance engineers who know more than I do.
June 2006	Have paying job in music industry. Have writing credits on at least four completed projects, whether paying or not. Have complete demo package prepared as writer/producer.

June 2007	Have at least one paying gig as writer/producer and enough contacts and knowledge to solicit business regularly.
June 2008	Support myself as a full-time writer/producer. ·

At any stage of your career, it's helpful to have a sense of what the next few years should look like. You'll see how the incremental progress you make every day contributes to significant progress in the long run. Build good habits into your schedule.

For example, you should plan to write every day, so that you are always improving your craft and keeping abreast of current styles. The best writers I've known all had the habit of writing daily. Also plan for regular research so that you always know what's current and what people are looking for—what skills you need to have, to support them. A daily and weekly calendar will help you to make time for these essential activities.

"Anthony," a successful writer I've known for a long time, came from a very successful business-oriented family. After he graduated from Berklee, he moved back home to Toronto. Every Wednesday, he'd get up early, brew a pot of coffee, and then spend the whole day on the phone. Anthony would introduce himself to companies, send out his demo package, network with musicians, and make follow-up calls. Gigs started coming in, and he did a killer job on them. Before long, he outgrew Toronto, and went to L.A. to make industrial films, and he's doing really great work.

By having this kind of schedule and recognizing that building a profitable business takes time, you will be encouraged by regularly achieving minor milestones, as they will assure you that you're on the right track. It's a critical part of the process.

PROJECT 1.1. WHAT'S YOUR TIMELINE?

What's your plan for opening shop as a writer/producer, or taking your existing writing business to the next level? Draft a timeline in as much detail as you can. Be realistic, but don't be afraid to dream. Show how to get from where you are to where you want to be.

Do this on a computer, so that it's easy to edit. You will be revising this timeline throughout the book—and throughout your career.

2. RESEARCH

Success as a writer depends on your knowledge of your local business landscape. You need to know where the gigs are, how to produce good quality products in your chosen genre, who the local musicians and studios are, and many other types of information. Research is a critical precursor to investing any money, and it's an ongoing activity. It takes time, and you need to devote yourself tirelessly to it.

The questions you will need to answer will vary between types of writing, and where you are in your career. For example, if you want to break into the jingle industry, you need to ask: What are the local big jingle houses? How are they doing it? Who are their clients? What do they charge? What is their quality standard?

Take the time to read business books and periodicals about the structure of the music industry. There is much great information about the music business, and I encourage you to find it. The best way is to network with successful individuals and companies and ask them about their perspectives and experiences. Here are some other sources of information.

Industry journals and magazines. Trade publications tell you what is going on in the industry, publish employment ads, and address the work that is currently available. There are countless trade magazines on the market for every specific type of commercial music. At the least, these journals will introduce you to the names of the most successful individuals in their respective fields. You will learn who is doing what, which companies are hiring them, and so on. Knowing as much as possible about your industry will increase your chances of success. Don't be afraid to contact these companies, no matter how large they may be. Be like Anthony, and spend every Wednesday on the phone. It's one of the finest investments you will ever make.

There are countless publications in the United States alone about each particular field. For example, if record production is your goal, *Billboard* magazine is a good choice. For film production—*Variety*; advice on mixing and engineering—*Mix* magazine . . . and so on. Research can lead you down a myriad of exciting paths.

People. Get in touch with all your current contacts in the writing genre and let them know you're around, available, and interested. These contacts could be your college peers, friends, colleagues of friends or other colleagues, or people you may have met at industry trade shows. In addition, you will be surprised at how helpful "strangers" can be in giving advice and direction. A great research technique is to talk to musicians who work for other companies. Find out what they have to say about the nature of the business and the people in it.

Online resources. An Internet search will easily lead you to a multitude of resources. For example, do an Internet search for "film music." Just a few of the search results include www.filmmusicmag. com, www.filmscoremonthly.com, www.cin3ma.tv, www.filmmusic. net, and www.filmmusic.com. There is enough information in those sites to keep you busy for days on end. In some cases, registration at good informational sites is free and sometimes includes both hard copy and online resource access.

Libraries. A trip to a major central library can yield numerous periodicals and publications that share your specific musical focus. Most large libraries subscribe to all of the key periodicals and journals. In addition, the waiting rooms of many production houses and recording studios have a large assortment of these publications available.

Industry events. Attend awards shows and trade shows, especially those in major centers for the industry—New York, Los Angeles, and Nashville. You will get a real feel for what is current and who is current. Huge trade shows such as NAMM (National Association of Music Merchandisers) can connect you with many people in all fields of the music industry. Attending trade shows in the related areas of your focus industry can also be informative. For example, any trade show focusing on computer gaming (and there are many of those) can introduce you to many people in the industry. Come armed with your stellar demo and promo package! Never stop planting those seeds.

Internships. A great way to learn about the writing/producing business is to take an internship at a successful company. Though most internships are unpaid, they help you experience how the business works, and will also give you the chance to meet people who share your goals—and who have achieved them. These relationships can lead to other opportunities, and many a great collaboration has evolved from an internship.

The younger you are and the fewer your familial obligations, the easier it is to do these gigs. If an internship makes sense for you, find one as soon as you can. If not, you may be able to assist or collaborate with another writer for just a project or two, to learn more about their field of specialty. And consider hiring someone to give you lessons in specific topics. Established writers commonly hire my more advanced students to help them to get the most out of new gear or software. These "reverse internships" can save you a lot of time.

PROJECT 1.2. CREATE YOUR RESEARCH PLAN

What do you need to know? How will you learn it?

List topics that you need to understand in order to become a higher-functioning writing professional. It might be helpful to also list topics that you do understand.

Do you have gaps in understanding technology? In financial budgeting? In knowing your local music scene? In communicating with people? List the topics you want a better handle on, and prioritize them. Then, list how you will learn about each one—what information sources will lead you the understanding you need.

Integrate your research plan into your timeline/calendar.

3. MISSION STATEMENT

After you've completed a bit of research, you will generally start to have an idea of what kind of work you want to do in the music industry. The next chapter discusses many possibilities. Music is written for all kinds of projects: jingles, videogames, corporate presentations, industrial training films, and more.

Pick a starting focus—something you really like. Dream! But pick just one, and focus your efforts there. It is possible that your career will lead you to other possibilities, but especially in the beginning, you'll have the best chance of success by trying to break into a single, narrow industry.

Then write a mission statement, articulating your focus. Keep it short. Some experts say that a mission statement should be about fourteen words long.

> *"Anthony Music is a music writing/production house that produces music for advertising jingles."*

Write it down, frame it, put it on your wall, and live by it. Channel all your marketing efforts there, until you exhaust all possibilities.

In this industry, a door may open into a hallway with another twenty doors. One day can change your life, and your direction can change on a dime.

One day you're writing, the next, you're a music supervisor, and the next, you're the music director for a Broadway show. Paths wind. It's how the business works, and it's how possibilities may come to you.

But change your essential focus only if you are absolutely positive you know what you are doing. A new mission statement is like a new company. Taking a gig or two outside your regular scope may be fine, but keeping your mission clear will help you to achieve your highest dreams and optimize your productivity.

Once you have your primary focus, it will help you to articulate your important goals and objectives. For example, do you want to have your own company or do you want to be an employee? Part of the process of determining your goals and objectives relies on a deep understanding of the field(s) you desire to enter.

PROJECT 1.3. MISSION STATEMENT

Write out your mission statement. Display it where it will be visible from your writing desk.

4. LOCATION

Once you've chosen a focus in the industry, choose a city. Nearly all major American film work is based in Los Angeles, and you'll be at a disadvantage if this is your chosen industry and you live somewhere else. A lot of records and commercial work is happening in L.A., New York, Nashville, and Chicago. Less is happening in other cities, and it will be harder for you to make a living there. There are some Internet-based music production houses; they tend to churn out a large number of small projects. Many writers would prefer a smaller number of more significant projects, but it might be worth it to you to choose a location over the type of work you do.

When you've settled in a city, focus your research on the industry's activity in that city. Get specific about where to site your office.

Visibility is essential. To get gigs, you need to make yourself known, so it's beneficial to set up your studio in a locale where music is happening. In many cities, there's an art area with ad agencies, film production houses, and recording studios clustered close together, like the Brill building in NY or the MuchMusic building in Toronto, with City Television and the National Film Board across the street. Find the vibrant place where artistic people have lunch, go for drinks, and walk down the street. Locate your studio where they meet each other and network.

Try to site even a small office right there, right in the heart of city. If you have the flexibility to choose your location, researching the ideal site will pay off.

PROJECT 1.4. LEARN YOUR REGION

Pick a city. Find five companies that specialize in the genre you articulated in your mission statement. Get on the phone, and interview them about the industry.

You can call other writers, potential clients, or anyone in the industry who might have some information that would be useful to you, as you start out.

Ask them about the business, in that area, and try to gain as much insight into it as you can.

My Berklee students do this as one of their assignments, and it is incredible what they get. Some people are positive, and some are frustrated. Some won't take their calls, which is something they need to get used to. Others talk their ears off. But if they get through, they find that people all have stories to tell, and they may offer you good insight into the state of the business where you're looking.

Once you have that, you'll be ready to make a strategy.

5. BUDGET

Business success as a writer/producer means making more money than you spend. If you get into debt, you'll likely feel forced to get any job to cover your payments, and that can kill the music for you. So you need to be extremely careful about your spending, and you need to have a realistic grasp on your income and expenses.

Here's another box I write on the whiteboard, for my students:

Be Realistic!

By being realistic, you will avoid situations that will force you into another career.

It's tough, especially at the beginning. Many writers start out with the burden of student loans, and without the benefit of contacts and job leads. It's even harder if you've got your own family to support. This career path isn't easy, and it requires a commitment of time and finances. There are only so many hours in a day, and if you are focused in other areas, you'll have difficulty doing what's necessary to make your career work.

But people are living successful careers as writers. Being careful about money is critical to success.

Keep a careful budget, itemizing your income and expenses. Live within it.

It may sound obvious, but it's important to wait to spend money on new gear until you have the money to pay for it. Gear is a place where it's easy to spend unnecessarily, and I've seen writers at all stages of their careers get into trouble by not keeping a careful enough accounting of their cash flow.

It's difficult to discuss what your income will be like. It varies so much, and different regions have different price points. To ballpark it very roughly, the bread and butter of a music writer's work comes from small projects that pay about $2,000 to $5,000, and are produced in the writer's home studio. Sometimes, larger projects turn up. Sometimes, we take smaller ones, if they are easily completed or are likely to lead to something bigger in the future. How many of these you'll get will vary, depending on how well connected you are.

Balance this against your expenses. Setting up a studio will be a large initial expense. It's difficult to do it for less than $4,000; $20,000 is better. But you need some way to record your music in a way that ultimately sounds professional.

Tracking all these finances is among the most critical business aspects of writing and producing. You need to supervise both the collection and distribution of funds and you must keep accurate records for tax purposes.

Good account books show your income, accounts payable (money you owe), and accounts receivable (money you're due). Get financial-management software for your computer, through which you can generate reports, categorize expenses, keep track of income, and generate checks. When your business gets rolling, a few hours a week will keep everything in order. This is an area you must diligently and regularly attend to.

Pay your taxes! Consider the scenario of a colleague of mine. He was making a lot of money as a commercial arranger and composer, but he was haphazard about managing his finances.

One year, with an accumulated income of more than $250,000 and no income tax return filed, the IRS finally contacted him. It turned out that he owed over $125,000 in taxes, penalties, and interest. He was forced to declare bankruptcy to avoid paying credit cards and other loans and leases. So, be careful. Always know where you stand financially.

When starting out, you will probably invest more back into your business than you will earn. If your business has been growing steadily and consistently, you will have the opportunity to move to the next level—maybe a larger office/studio in a nicer location, some new equipment, or perhaps an employee to help with the books. All of these things help your company grow in stature and income, but be conservative and cautious in your thinking. It is the music business, after all, and anything can happen.

When you accept a job, if appropriate, include a clause in your contract to receive a deposit before the job starts that can cover some expenses. Even a small sum is important as a way of getting a commitment, and enables you to pay some of your bills before you receive full payment from your client.

In the corporate world, where invoices have to be sent to the appropriate financial departments, it is common practice to give your client thirty days to pay off a balance. However, corporations often take longer, sometimes up to 90–120 days. Sometimes, if you agree in writing, you can reduce the fee marginally (2–3 percent) to get a payment a little quicker. However, this is not a good idea unless your cash flow is low. If you are doing a recording session using members of AFM (American Federation of Musicians), AFTRA (American Federation of Television and Radio Artists), or SAG (Screen Actors Guild), check with the union to find out the time frame for submitting payment for individual types of work. Many times, the funds are sent to the union, which then disburses the funds to the players. The deadlines to submit payment to the musicians and vocalists in AFM, AFTRA, and SAG usually are ten to fifteen days following the recording session.

If you become busy and these financial matters become too time consuming, hire a billing service, of which there are many. They work for many production houses, distributing and keeping track of payments. They also ensure that the proper taxes, health and welfare, and pension and welfare contributions to appropriate unions are deducted and paid. Often, they can also take care of paying union dues, work dues, and commissions. Billing services typically charge a handling fee of 3–10 percent of the gross amount being handled, but it can save your company money and worry, since you wouldn't need to hire an accountant.

The bottom line is that you need clear financial records. It is a key to having a successful business. Details of financial management are beyond the scope of this book, but it is critical that you have a handle on it, if you are to have a career as a writer.

PROJECT 1.5. BUILD YOUR BUDGET

Build your budget. List your income and expenses, your assets, and your debts. What should you be saving for?

Is your spending appropriate for your financial situation?

FORMAL BUSINESS PLANS

Creating a formal business plan will give you direction as you begin your career, help you to focus your finances, and provide necessary documentation if you seek outside funding such as loans or investors.

Your business will likely take the form of a **production house**. A production house is the name given to any business that produces commercial music, and can range in size from an individual with a basic hard disk–based recording setup to a large company with many employees and multiple large-format studios.

Whether large or small, however, it is still a business, and to succeed, you need a plan. Even if you are the only person who will ever see this plan, don't skip this step. Writing the plan will help you to articulate your goals and set a path to achieving them. A solid business plan contains the key components listed below. (Each element is discussed further in coming chapters.)

The more specific you are in writing your plan, the more prepared you will be for success. Get a good book on writing a business plan. Look up "sample business plans" or "writing a business plan" using any respected Internet search engine; you'll find plenty of helpful and free resources.

ELEMENTS OF A BUSINESS PLAN

Executive Summary

The executive summary presents a concise and brief description of your company's goals and achievements. If your company is new, then include a compelling description of your own professional achievements and academic accomplishments, followed by a statement of how effective your production house will be as a result. The words "dedicated" and "committed" are always powerful. If possible, an impressive description of the company's accomplishments can also be very potent. A list of major clients, along with references, gives a positive impression to your potential clients.

The executive summary should not be too long—ideally, no longer than one page. If your summary extends past two pages, consider deleting some information. If you need (or want) to include more detail about your business or yourself, add a longer description at the end of the business plan.

Business Background

The Company

A concise summary of your company, including your background and how you came to this business. Also, describe the business structure (sole proprietorship, corporation, or partnership).

The Service

Descriptions of what services you provide and their key selling features.

Key Personnel

If your business is a sole proprietorship, this is a paragraph about you. If it's a partnership, this covers you and your business partner(s).

Marketing Plans

Market Analysis

What is the scope of the market for writer/producers? Where is all the work, geographically? Who's hiring writer/producers? Where is the need? Use your research.

Marketing Strategy

How do you plan to market your business? This should be detailed. How will you make new contacts? Will you advertise? How often and where? Will you network? With whom? How much will you spend on marketing materials, such as brochures, a promotional kit, a Web site, and other materials?

Pricing Strategy

How much will you charge? If you are not sure, the phrase "competitively priced" is always safe and leaves room for negotiation. Recognize your worth, but be fair. It is important to research and get a feel for what your competitors are charging.

Business Considerations

Income

Indicate your projected sources of revenue and income expected from each. You can briefly discuss what other writer/producers earn, and how they have made their livings. What's your specialty?

Expenses

How much will the business cost to run? What are the start-up costs and what is the overhead? Calculate your monthly living expenses, including rent, food, clothes, travel, entertainment, utilities, and loan payments. Once you have calculated your living costs, factor in *every penny* you spend on your writing and production company. This gives you an idea of how much you need to live and keep your company going. Also, how will your profits be dispersed? Will they go back into the company (equipment, infrastructure, promotion, etc.), into savings, or to the owners?

Operations

Who will manage the business aspects? You or an accountant? How will you collect payment and pay contractors?

Space and Equipment: Computer, Office, Studio

Where will your business operate? In your house? In an office or studio? How much will you need to spend for computer equipment, music-production software and effects, office supplies, and building a studio? What will you need to purchase? Be specific, listing what you already have and finding cost estimates for each item that you don't.

INDUSTRY SPOTLIGHT: PARTNERSHIPS

The idea of a partnership deserves serious attention, and it is commonplace for producers to form them. Though I've said that writer/producers need to be all things to all people, it may be more realistic and practical for you to bring in a business partner. A list of potential candidates for partnership for a writer might be:

- a studio owner or recording engineer or both
- a person who is excellent at business promotion and networking and who is motivated to start and promote a writing and production house
- a lyricist, if you don't write lyrics
- a person who has a particular writing strength or experience you don't possess
- a person involved in multimedia
- a screenwriter or ad writer
- someone with capital who is willing to back your business
- a programmer or computer expert, if this is not your forte
- another writer who plays a variety of instruments that you don't
- a person connected to another field of the music business who can diversify and augment the scope of your work

Without exception, a partnership should begin in writing with a legal contract prepared by a lawyer. Business books will tell you a lot about the legalities of working with a partner—and most of them apply to the music industry. But remember that the music industry has specific issues of its own, and the most important of these are copyright issues. Be sure that you have written agreements delineating who owns copyrights and publishing rights, and who is entitled to income from copyrights, both in the short term and the long term.

PROJECT 1.6. CREATE A BUSINESS PLAN

Create a business plan for your writing business. Assemble components that exist already, and plan how you will create those that are missing.

- Executive Summary (includes mission statement)
- Background of the Company, its Service, and Key Personnel Bios

- Marketing Strategy
- Pricing Strategy
- Budget Projections: Predicted Income vs. Expenses
- Operations
- Space and Equipment
- Calendar

Be sure to answer these questions:

- What is your strategy for the next year?
- What major expenses are coming? How will you finance them?

CONCLUSION

Our goal is to spend as much of our time as possible writing music. By being methodical in setting up and running your business, you will be able to focus more on how you want to spend your time. There is freedom in good organization, and it will be well worth your while to attend carefully to the business aspects of your writing endeavors.

CHAPTER **2**

Opportunities for Writing Music

THERE HAVE NEVER BEEN AS MANY DIFFERENT WAYS to make a living by writing music as there are today. As technology evolves to support new kinds of media, and as multimedia communications become more common, new music is increasingly in demand.

The traditional opportunities in writing for commercials, radio, television, and film all continue to exist. Additionally, and increasingly, companies are adding music to presentations, training films, and Web sites. Cell phones and other portable electronic devices have unique ring tones and other sounds. Videogame scores are often more elaborate than film scores, and often more lucrative for their creators. And, of course, there's songwriting. Where some opportunities are in decline, such as writing for live theater, new opportunities for writing are continually emerging, such as music for Web pages and for music libraries.

The musical landscape is ever changing, and the relative opportunities in these areas will vary. Making a living as a freelance writer/producer requires versatility and flexibility, so you'll need to learn to write for a variety of applications. In this chapter, I'll discuss many of these different possibilities and the differences in how they work. The "Resources" list at the end of this book will point you towards more information on many of them.

COMMERCIALS

Television and radio commercials require theme music and sometimes lyrics for advertising applications, jingles, and underscores. Companies of all sizes use commercials. Larger companies might have an internal marketing and promotions department that produces their commercials, with in-house creative directors among their stable of copywriters, art directors, and producers—many of whom may be the music writer's contact. Many companies use outside advertising agencies to produce their promotional campaigns.

Ads need to stay current, and they often reflect music being used in Hollywood films and on the popular-music charts. To appeal to producers of commercials, you need to stay current with popular culture.

Rather than commissioning new music, some companies (particularly smaller businesses) will use *library music*—pre-produced music that can be purchased. This is less expensive, but also less customized and original. Furthermore, a current trend is to license popular music, especially hit songs, to support a product image.

Over the years, TV commercials have shrunk from a minute to thirty seconds, and more recently, down to fifteen seconds. At a minute long, jingles were more like miniature songs. Today, the original music required is more like an underscore, usually in support of a voiceover.

In addition to advertising jingles, radio and TV stations use music for other functions: IDs, stingers, bumpers, and other musical tidbits.

Whether at an in-house marketing/promotion department or an independent ad agency, the procedure for obtaining commercial work is similar. Producers keep phone numbers for several music writers on hand. When music is needed, they call several who are likely to be appropriate and request demos, usually in a very tight time frame, such as a couple days. They choose the best demo and then award the contract to that writer.

The writer then produces the final version. The contracted writer composes the music, sets up and oversees the recording session, possibly engineers and mixes the session, and then delivers the final product. At larger companies, the writer's task is sometimes more focused on just writing, without production responsibilities. Smaller projects, though, tend to be all inclusive.

Similar to commercials are public service announcements. These are generally produced by not-for-profit organizations to endorse an idea or cause, such as political issues, humanitarian projects, and general community service needs. Though budgets for such projects are often too small to include music, providing music to them for free is a good way to gain some experience and build your portfolio.

FILM

As a **film and television writer/producer**, you will most likely work very closely with the director and/or music supervisor of the project. Beforehand, you present a series of demos or rough sequences to illustrate the musical direction. The music supervisor and director make the ultimate decision as to whether your compositions are appropriate for the visual and discuss any changes with you. When it comes time to record the music, you are responsible for the production of the artistic areas right through to the mixes.

Many kinds of films are made, from full-featured Hollywood-style films to smaller industrial, or educational films, to TV movies. From a composer's perspective, there are many similarities between them.

Film music includes many different types of cues. There are main themes, underscores that support action and sometimes dialog, and music for credits. Sometimes, *source music* is used—music that comes from a musical element or device in the story or setting, such as a radio playing or a character singing in the shower. This music may be pre-existing or it may be original.

The music supervisor will generally coordinate the music, and possibly create a temp score, to be used as a reference during the production process. The director will have the final approval over the music. The director, music supervisor, and writer may all sit down to a *spotting session* before the music is created, to look at the scenes and determine where music will be used and what type of music it should be.

Depending on the film's budget, there may be separate individuals in charge of engineering, mixing, mastering, and even orchestration. On small-budget films, a writer may be responsible for production as well.

Working on small independent films and student films is a good way to begin work in this industry, to gain experience and credentials. Large-budget Hollywood film projects are the domain of a small number of highly experienced, well-known individuals. TV documentaries and movies include a wider group.

There are many more opportunities for work in commercial training films, which are produced by large companies. The writing process is like that of entertainment films, and the networking process is more like in commercial work; writers of commercial/industrial shows and films often work with larger film-production companies. One difference in films for corporations is that some of the music for their branding may already exist and require rearranging or using it in its original form. These films are generally released on DVD, often to be used exclusively in-house for employee training, sales presentations, and corporate promotion, rather than to general-public release. This type of work can be very lucrative.

Live theater productions are a relatively small market, but you may find that opportunities exist for you. The musical requirements are much like film, though there are frequently instrumental pieces necessary during scene changes. The opening theme may be replaced by an overture, and the closing credits replaced by an intro recap. Underscores—supportive music behind picture or dialogue—tend to be less common, particularly under dialog, due to the engineering requirements of live sound.

TELEVISION PROGRAMS

Television programs also use music in many ways, and are similar in process to filmmaking. There is a lot of work available, given the enormous number of cable television and network stations.

Every program has an opening and closing theme. Throughout the program are underscores, source music, and also *bumpers*, which are used to connect scenes or camera shots. If the TV show already exists, then the themes will be written already. The new music will be primarily the underscore.

Like film, television is a relatively collaborative process, with oversight of the music by a director and music supervisor. But in television, music writers are more often responsible for the final production.

RECORDINGS

Songwriting for other performers remains a vast opportunity for creating music. Singer/songwriters sometimes engage other writers to assist with arranging, development of ideas, and to serve as objective listeners/collaborators. And, of course, many writers perform their own work.

Recordings are generally overseen by producers, who are often the artists themselves. A producer may try to find songs that are appropriate for an artist's album.

Currently, sales of music online are increasing dramatically, while CD sales are declining. To paraphrase David Kusek and Gerd Leonard in their book *The Future of Music* (Berklee Press, 2005; futureofmusicbook.com), it's a lousy time for the record industry but a great time for the music industry. More artists are producing more songs now than at any other time in history.

While most music writing projects are paid on a per-project basis, with no royalties or residuals, songwriting tends to be royalty based (see chapter 4).

As a **record producer,** you oversee the entire artistic and recording process. The producer's amount of artistic input varies from artist to artist. For example, it's highly likely that Daniel Lanois had broad artistic input in the creation of Peter Gabriel's album *So*. In some cases, the producer's role is to be the objective listener, while the artist records the music that he or she envisions. When artists such as the Police, Sting, and Phil Collins used Hugh Padgham to produce their records, one can easily surmise Hugh Padgham's engineering had a lot to do with the final sound. One thing is consistent among all great producers: they are instrumental in creating a unique, high-quality, and recognizable sound for their artists.

In many cases, particularly in the earlier days of recording, the producer was the liaison between the artist and the record company. Staff producers such as Voyle Gilmore and Lee Gillette were employees of Capitol Records and produced artists such as Frank Sinatra, Nat King Cole, and Peggy Lee. An example of a complete producer is Tony Brown, former president of MCA Nashville. His production responsibilities are enormous, entailing every aspect of the record-making process.

MULTIMEDIA

Multimedia applications may represent the largest set of opportunities for music writers in the near future. The videogame industry is currently larger than the film industry, in terms of dollars. Computer and networking technology is increasing at such a fast pace that likely music for Web pages will become a major new source for work, in the coming years. Corporate presentations, like PowerPoint versions of industrial training films, are also using music now and some composers are finding great opportunities in that type of work.

Multimedia applications include videogames, Web sites, educational tools, business applications, and a growing number of additional areas. This type of work calls for expertise in a multitude of musical genres and knowledge of many processes, from composition to final product delivery. The newest video game developers look for composers to be primarily film-type composers to match the latest game styles and realistic animation.

Primary contacts tend to be creative directors at software companies, and you may work very closely with the software programmers, and create cues to very exacting specifications. Musical elements such as loops are particularly common in this type of work.

This industry is very large and growing quickly.

SOUND DESIGN AND OTHER SPECIAL APPLICATIONS

A small but growing industry is in designing sounds for products such as computer action sounds, cellphone ring tones, PDAs, themes for PA announcements in public places, and other special applications. Like commercial work, these are generally managed by the creative director/manager within the product manufacturer's staff. You might work closely with a technical team on this type of music. Writers generally must produce the final product, which frequently includes special knowledge of compression technologies, working with limited bandwidths, and loops.

COMMERCIAL MUSIC LIBRARIES

As a writer/producer of music for commercial music libraries, you compose music of all styles, lengths, and orchestrations, to be included on CDs that are sold to radio stations, television studios, advertising agencies, and other companies producing their own multimedia projects. The company that produces these CDs is considered your "client." There are two common models. In one, the end user pays a lot for each CD, but can use the music royalty free. In the other, the CDs are relatively inexpensive, but the end user pays to license the music that they actually use. The writer/producer typically receives a one-time payment, but occasionally receives a small payment for each use.

This type of work generally involves delivery of a final recording. Musical versatility is a must. Your contact will be the owners or creative directors for music-library companies. This industry is quite large and a good starting point for beginning writers.

Though music from libraries is being used in place of music specifically constructed for individual creative projects, the libraries are employing the writers now, so overall, the jobs still exist.

PROJECT 2.1. FIND MODELS IN YOUR GENRE

What area of music writing appeals to you? Choose one, and then find five excellent examples of that kind of work. Look at them carefully. Why were they successful? Then produce your own music that would have also fulfilled those projects. Use the models as a guide, but make your own music different enough that you can use it on your demo recordings.

For an added challenge, try the same process in as many other areas as you can find. Choose models and imitate them. You may find that other possibilities are surprisingly appealing.

CONCLUSION

When you're starting out, choose a focus, and stick to it. This will help you strategize your marketing efforts. If you decide on composing TV commercials, and then a film-scoring gig falls into your lap, you can take it, but realize that it's distracting you from what might be your preferred area. Then again, you might decide that you enjoy it more than jingle work and then change direction. That's fine, but again, focus your marketing on just one area, to get the most for your efforts.

CHAPTER 3

Finding Work

ONCE YOU'VE CHOSEN A WORK GENRE AND ARE COMFORTABLE with your business strategy, it's time to find paying projects. You'll need materials related to your business identity: a company name, business cards, letterhead, Web site, and so on, but the centerpiece of your marketing efforts will be your demo recording. In this chapter, we'll look at the materials and process of finding work writing music. This boils down to creating your demo and shopping it around.

It's not always the best writers who consistently get hired. It's the writers who can deliver a great product in a professional manner.

When a prospective client makes a decision regarding which writer to go with, they listen to the writer's demo recording and then they trust their instinct about whether they think the writer will be easy to work with. Credentials that might be important to you will often be irrelevant to who is hiring you for a project. Prospective clients just want to hear your work and to be assured that they can count on you to deliver what they need on time.

Writing good music is like any other musical skill. Practice makes perfect. Study, emulate, write, and record. Your standard will always be what the most successful writers are producing. That's your benchmark; don't settle for less. It is beyond the scope of this book to talk about composition techniques, but learn from the masters.

YOUR IDENTITY

Prospective clients who don't know you will examine every object you put before them, trying to piece together enough information about you to make an informed hiring decision.

Imagine a client sending out a call for demos for music to under-score a TV commercial. They have narrowed the field to two poten-tial demos and they like both equally. One CD has a laser-printed label, clearly indicating the writer's contact information. The other has something illegibly scribbled on it with a Sharpie. The writer who does the clear labels will be perceived as the more professionally accomplished and may be considered most likely to deliver a final product on time. This judgment has nothing to do with the quality of music. But it is the reality of how decisions get made.

All your communications with your client, from your company name to how quickly and politely you answer their calls, will contribute to their overall impression of whether you will be a good music provider to them or not. So invest in developing materials that project a professional image.

You need an established identity. Your company name is very important. It should be unique and represent you and your business. Companies like Microsoft, Konami, and Dreamworks have names that industry people can easily remember. As your business grows, the name will become synonymous with your high-quality work.

Once you have this, you can develop your promotional mate-rials—business cards, brochures, fliers, promotional package, and demo recording. All need to look consistent and support your busi-ness objectives. Likely, you'll need help with this. If you know a graphic designer, it's a good time to ask for help in designing a logo and other graphics.

Your marketing research will indicate who your prospective clients are. Direct your advertising and promotion materials to those individuals and companies. Regardless of your target market, prepare yourself with great-sounding demos, dynamic print ads, promo kits, and other materials that present your music and your business in a powerful and memorable way. Don't forget the fridge magnets!

Do whatever you can to promote yourself professionally. Part of your research should include investigating the promotional materials of your competition. Develop an outstanding Web site. Attend trade shows. Find out where the artistic people hang out and network with them. Set up introductory business meetings and personally deliver your promotional kit to each of your new contacts. Meeting potential clients in person demonstrates how important their business is to you.

CONTACTS

Getting work in the music business relies very much on who you know and who knows you. It's a networking business. Many jobs are not even advertised, but rather get communicated by word of mouth. The challenge in the music industry, then, is getting to know the right people.

First, you need to be findable. Make sure your company name is in the phone book and your Web site is registered with all the online search engines.

Then assemble a list of names and numbers of the people who are the decision makers in the target companies you've been researching: the people who deal with and hire writers. If you know anyone with connections inside these companies, see if they can introduce you to whoever hires music writers. If you don't know anyone, you'll have to make a cold call.

Introduce yourself and be ready to speak knowledgeably about their company and their work. (Your research will have given you this information.) Try to get a one-on-one personal meeting. If you have a nice office setup, invite your clients to listen to your work and see your facility. If not, offer to meet them at their office. Establish personal contact and then sell yourself and your work. Follow up the call by sending your promotional kit. A week or two after sending the promo kit, call again to see if it has been received and listened to. Set aside several hours a week just to make telephone calls. Cold calls can be difficult to make, but they are a necessary part of any business. Be confident and make the call.

CREATING A PROMO KIT

Your promo kit is a set of documents and recordings that you send to prospective clients. With some modifications, it can also be used as a "press kit," which you can send to radio stations or newspapers, if you are trying to get publicity. In this book, we'll use the term "promo kit," as its purpose here is to get writing jobs, and is therefore promoting your company. Performing musicians are more inclined to use press kits.

Here are the principal ingredients of a writer/producer's promo kit:

- **Cover letter introducing yourself and your company, on company letterhead.** If the potential client has asked for your promotional material, the cover letter expresses how grateful you are for their interest in your work. Communicate to them that you are the right choice to fill all of their musical needs. This is a necessary part of the kit, but it shouldn't be long.
- **A biography or a brochure.** This is optional, but often included. Describe your services, but be succinct. Keep your bio to *one page*. A brochure is an effective way to get your message across. It can be just a single page, tri-fold, and printed on glossy paper. Include information that will entice potential clients. Stress that your original music will bring character and quality to their product. "Custom-made" is a powerful phrase. Stress that your music is custom-made for them and their product—assuming that it is.
- **Demo CD, DVD, or video.** This is the most important part of the promo kit, and it *must* be outstanding. The demo gives your potential clients an idea of your capabilities as a writer, engineer, producer, and performer. It provides examples of how your music fits into a particular genre or how versatile you are at writing for different media. Your music demo should be on CD and well packaged, or even better, on an enhanced CD with film, jingle, or multimedia clips that your music has accompanied. Ensure that both the CD and insert contain all of your contact information, in case they get separated.
- **Testimonials from colleagues, former and present clients, and awards.** Start keeping a file of all of the positive letters that you receive, and include copies in the promo kit. These are not necessary to include, but may be helpful to support your case.
- **Reviews, articles, or promotions in which you are mentioned or that you have written.** Include samples of any media coverage you have received, work you have done in other music-related fields such as engineering or performing, work you have done as an employee of another production house or partnership in the past, and articles you have written. Again, this is not a necessary component, but may help.
- **Follow-up phone call(s).** This is so important to self-promotion that I consider it a part of the promotion kit.

Every press kit you send should be followed by a personal phone call. The telephone is one of the most important "instruments" that you have to learn in the music business. Of course, the best way to attract clients is to talk to them in person. This develops a personal rapport and gives you a true sense of what individuals are thinking and how they are responding to what you have to offer them.

Most writers today have Web sites that mirror their promo kits. These are essentially online versions of the same materials. A Web site can have more information, such as links to commercial recordings, photographs, and such, but the essentials should be easily accessible.

MORE ABOUT DEMOS

Demos are created for specific projects and clients. Until relatively recently, demos were basic recordings. The final product might be an orchestra, but the demo would be a very rough version, to give the client an idea of what the final product might sound like.

Today's demos are much more polished. They are practically final versions, usually completed with minor feedback from the client. The sound must be professional quality, with most of the instruments likely to appear on the final version. Modern MIDI and sample-based recording processes make this feasible in a way that was impossible twenty years ago, but that's the state of the industry, and always expected by potential clients.

There are two types of demos: one for the jobs you want, and the other for the jobs you have.

The jobs you want: There are typically several other writers competing for the same job, so your demo must stand out. In most cases, all writers competing for a job receive the same creative information and specifications, and are asked to submit demos. Some examples of demos needed for competition might be:

- An advertising agency is looking for a jingle for a new campaign. It wants to choose from several music production houses that submit demo jingles.
- A film production company wants a composer to compose the score for its newest film. The theme has already been written and the synchronization licenses have been obtained

for the film's music, which is to be period music—designed
to mimic a particular era. As the budget is tight, the company
is looking for a smaller company to do this work and is audi-
tioning several writers by having them all write for one scene.
The director and music supervisor will choose the writer they
feel is best suited.

- A large radio-station group is producing a set of station IDs
  for its adult-contemporary stations nationwide. These short
  pieces of music, which state the radio station's call numbers
  and name, are key to the station's identity, and the group has
  engaged a music agency to find a writer for all of these spots.
  The agent is soliciting demos from various music composers
  and companies.
- A new jingle production house is looking for staff writers.

The purpose of these demos is to show your capabilities, creating
music exactly like that needed by the client.

The job you have: When writing and producing demos for
jobs you have been hired for, the clients have already acknowledged
that your services are what they need. The demo provides an example
of the work you've done to meet the client's particular creative needs.
A few specific examples might be:

- A television production house wants you to write music for
  a trailer that it will be using to promote a show. Your agreement stipulates that you have to write the music for all of
  the show's promo clips, and the production house wants
  to hear demos before finalizing the tracks. In this case, you
  would write the music and produce it to fit the picture. The
  director or music supervisor listens to the demo versions and,
  most often, requires that changes be made. If the tracks were
  produced on the computer, you can produce the final version
  with the knowledge that the piece is acceptable when the final
  approval is given.
- A record company has hired you to produce one of its artists.
  The artist has a raw song that has a great hook, but needs
  a lot of work. The record company wants to hear the demo
  of your ideas before they approve the next step of entering
  the recording studio. In fact, this is *preproduction* and can
  really assist in making the actual recording of the album flow
  smoothly, because many of the musical ideas will have been

formulated beforehand. This is popular with many labels; it gives them more financial control and keeps the costs down.

- An ad agency has hired you to write and produce music for a series of commercials over a period of time. The music in these ad spots, all for television, is a focal point of the campaign. Before each phase, the agency wants to hear your music so that it can make any suggestions.
- A museum has hired you to write the music for a multimedia presentation on art in the Renaissance period. The producers of the documentary want to hear the authenticity of the writing before they approve your budget for a recording using Renaissance instruments.

In producing a demo, your primary goals are to compose well-crafted and memorable music that works with the visuals, if applicable, and to submit a *great-sounding* recording that is impressive on the first listen and represents what you are capable of doing. In many cases, demos will create your reputation.

If you are just starting out and haven't done any professional work yet, find talented young filmmakers and offer to write music for their soundtracks. Choose a variety of different genres and put them in an order that makes a powerful presentation. If your presentation includes musical excerpts not written to picture, add some kind of multimedia presentation, maybe featuring glossy photos of your studio or graphic displays of interest.

Make sure that the packaging of your demos looks professional. Compact disks and DVDs are now the industry standard. They should have printed labels and arrive in jewel cases. Files are also exchanged via FTP. Draft MP3s are sometimes sent via e-mail.

PROJECT 3.1. MARKETING MATERIALS

Assemble your marketing materials, and develop a plan for any items you don't have.

- You need items related to your identity: business name, logo, business cards, letterhead, envelopes, mailing labels, CD labels.
- You need a press kit: cover letter, bio, brochure, testimonials, reviews, recordings, photos.

- You will create customized demo CDs, DVDs, etc., for each kit, but you should keep a library of past work on hand, in case anyone requests additional samples.
- You will need a Web site, which may include additional materials, such as links to your work, photos, and so on.

MARKETING COLLABORATORS

Marketing is a vast field, and to do it right, you'll likely be best served by finding some gifted collaborators to help you get work. We already mentioned graphic designers. You also might hire someone to do your Web site. Just as contemporary music writers are often working as their own recording engineers, graphic designers today are often also working to design Web sites. Other people you might find yourself collaborating with in the process of finding work are agents and lawyers.

AGENTS

Another potential way to identify and obtain jobs, in addition to having impressive promotional materials and a great demo, is to secure an agent to represent you. There are music agents in most major cities to represent writers and composers, particularly for film and television work. Agents are not generally used in advertising music. Find agents who specialize in promoting music in your field, and arrange meetings with them. However, realize that securing an agent is often difficult. Even if an agent doesn't take you on as a client, he or she can give you great insight into the business and tell you who is working, why they are working, and who is hiring.

Normally, agents charge a percentage of your gross pay, usually 15 to 20 percent. That figure can vary according to the agreement you make. When seeking out agents, investigate their experience, fields of expertise, and existing clients, as well as their reputation for stability and integrity. If an agent takes you on as a client, he or she should believe in your work. Speak with your agent as often as you can, and look for results.

If you find an agent who is willing to take you on as a client, it is important that you first get legal advice from a lawyer before signing *anything*. Lawyers are not inexpensive, but the money you spend on one, although it may seem steep in the beginning, can save a fortune in the end. The contract between you and the agent will specify the responsibilities of both you and the agent.

LAWYERS

There are many times in your career when you'll need some kind of help and advice from the legal profession. It may be to negotiate a record contract, set up personal-services contracts, or prepare standardized contracts for general use.

Make sure that you use an **entertainment lawyer**. Entertainment lawyers know the business and how to reach the right people. They'll know how far to push and when to hold up, and they are legally and ethically obligated to negotiate in *your* best interest.

Shop around for a fair, honest, and reputable entertainment lawyer. Entertainment lawyers are specialists and are generally expensive. Don't employ a generic real estate/divorce/personal injury lawyer in hopes of saving a few dollars. You won't get the same results.

A good place to start is to ask colleagues for recommendations. Speak to several lawyers about their billing practices, fee schedules, retainer fees, previous experience, availability, and their willingness to moderate *your* spending. Here are some good questions to ask:

- How much experience do you have in the entertainment field?
- What are your standard fees (for specific services)?
- What are your payment terms?
- Who are your current clients?
- What are your specific areas of expertise?
- What professional organizations are you affiliated with?

Watching Your Legal Costs

Some lawyers can run up costs very quickly with phone calls, photocopies and faxes, couriers, unnecessary meetings, and the like. They keep a docket, and you are entitled to a detailed account of every penny you are being charged. Do as much of the work as you can yourself. When talking to your lawyer, keep the calls brief. Some lawyers have a ten- or fifteen-minute minimum for phone calls. Don't call your lawyer unless it is absolutely necessary, and leave concise detailed messages rather than lengthy and costly exposés. Offer to photocopy necessary documents yourself. The five cents per copy at your local office-supply stores will most likely be much cheaper than the rates at the law office.

Have the lawyer's office mail any documents via regular mail and not via expensive couriers. Ensure that your lawyer agrees to allow you to attend any meetings, making sure they are at your lawyer's office, so you are not saddled with paying the lawyer's travel costs.

COMMUNICATING WITH CLIENTS

Once you've sent the promotional kit, made your follow-up calls, and scheduled a meeting, you must prepare to meet your clients. You can only make a first impression once, so make it a good one. Here are some tips:

- Have a professional portfolio on hand for presentation to potential new clients. Bring extra copies, just in case they are needed.
- Learn about the people and the companies your clients work for before you first meet them.
- Have your meetings in a place conducive to the nature of the project.
- Be more concerned about what you can do for them than what they can do for you.
- Never criticize your competition or your client's competition.
- Be confident in your own abilities: don't sell yourself short, but don't sound arrogant.
- Leave your clients with the impression that you are a very hard worker.
- Avoid appearing to be desperate for work. For example, sending several demos for a project might be interpreted as a sign of desperation.

If your musical productions live up to the professional image you present, job opportunities will follow.

FIVE STEPS TO GOOD CLIENT RELATIONSHIPS

You have to create your own niche and do so in a smart and businesslike manner. Here are some tips. They may seem obvious, but in my experience, it's often the most obvious things that escape attention. Periodically review this list to keep on your toes.

1. **Present a professional image.** Your appearance is a reflection of who you are as a person and as a professional. If you are organized and care about your appearance, your clients will likely believe that you are also this way in your writing/production life.

2. **Communicate clearly.** One of the greatest challenges you will have in both the business and artistic ends of production is dealing with non-musician clients. They may be advertising people, record-company executives, or film directors and producers. Often these people will speak a different "language" than you. If you don't understand what they are saying, ask for clarification. Try to avoid using obscure musical terms. Do your best to speak in their terms and language.

3. **The client is right.** Listen carefully and with sensitivity to what your client is saying. Even if you are aware that what they are asking for is difficult or even impossible to deliver, allow meaningful dialog. You can then describe with diplomacy and understanding how their concept might not work for their project. Take their idea and build on it. For example, phrases like, "That's a great idea and we could take that a step further by . . ." can work very well.

   If the client wants something specific, you should be pleased to provide this musical service. If he or she is adamant about music in a style with which you are not familiar, be encouraging—but then go right to the nearest record shop and buy as many records in that style as you can afford. Research, research, research! You'll be an expert in a matter of hours.

4. **Know your limits.** Don't overextend yourself or put yourself in a position to make your product sound bad or unprofessional. Know your capabilities and your limitations, and never promise the client anything that you can't deliver at the highest quality. You're better off saying "no" than delivering a substandard product.

5. **Don't bash the competition.** This kind of approach might win the small battle, but it'll never win the war. The music business is small and your current client might be

inclined to think, "If he says that about my competition, what is he going to say about me?" Furthermore, one day you might be looking to work for the very person you have been putting down.

PROJECT 3.2. LIST YOUR CONTACTS

Who do you know that will likely help you in your career? List potential client contacts and potential collaborators, including lawyers, agents, marketing/promotional people, graphic designers, Web site developers, musicians, engineers, and so on. If it's not a long list, how will you meet more people who could potentially help you?

When you have your marketing materials set, and a sample promo kit ready, is there someone on this list who would be likely to give you constructive feedback?

CONCLUSION

The methodology of finding work will change, as the industry evolves. Twenty years ago, I would have recommended that you submit a cassette demo. Today, reputation, CDs, DVDs, and Web sites are important aspects of finding work, and in ten years from now, the industry standard might be something else entirely. But one thing will remain the same: writers are successful because they work hard and believe in what they are doing. They are always on the top of their game—networking, constantly writing and improving their craft, staying current with new technologies, getting demos out, and producing a great product. They are also easy to work with, and genuinely serve their clients well. This will never change. The jobs *are* there. If you are proactive about finding them, and about projecting a professional image, you will be poised to succeed.

Business smarts are equally as important as artistic mastery. They go hand in hand to make a successful career.

You need to be comfortable talking to people, in person. Especially now, in our age of e-mails, faxes, and other long-distance communications, the face-to-face meeting is very powerful. Try to meet decision makers in person. They will be much more likely to hire you.

CHAPTER **4**
Getting Paid

AT FIRST, THE JOBS YOU ATTRACT will most likely be low budget and inconsistent. Don't get discouraged! Just as you wouldn't stop practicing your instrument even if you weren't doing any gigs, you must not stop perfecting your writing and production craft. You have to continue to dedicate yourself to a level of top-notch professionalism in both art and business. This will lead to newer and better demos, more recognition for your efforts, and ideally, more income.

It can be tricky to evaluate how much you're worth, but in negotiations, you need to separate your business self from your artistic self. You are self-employed and ultimately determine the value of your time, work, and talent by how much you charge.

Even at the outset of your career, you must set a value on your time and work, if only charging a token fee. If you will be working for no fee on a project but your client will be getting paid, you should consider your involvement in the project. Reward may not always be monetary. There may be times, especially when you're starting out, that you choose to work for free in exchange for other benefits, such as portfolio building, other kinds of credit, important contacts, or exposure. If this is the case, weigh the situation and potential benefits very carefully before agreeing to work for nothing. Working for nothing can send the message that the value of your time and work is just that: nothing.

Protect your right to earn a fair salary commensurate with your ability and experience. Setting a value on your work can be determined by asking yourself a series of questions:

- What are other writer/producers in your peer group getting for the same work?

- What is the hourly rate you will be comfortable working for? Make sure to estimate an appropriate amount of hours to complete the job.
- What is the dollar figure you place on your rising "marquis" value?
- How much are your production and performance skills worth and what kind of hourly value do you place on your home-studio setup? The more value your studio has and the better it sounds, the larger the hourly rate should be.
- What is the client's budget?
- What is the project timeline? When the project is due yesterday, adjust your fees accordingly.

In setting your price, remember to deduct 30 percent for taxes to realize your net fee and allow for your costs: overhead in equipment, musicians' and artists' fees, and other expenses.

I hate "ballparking" real numbers for what writers get paid, as it varies so much, depending on so many factors. People ask me this all the time, so I'll provide a rough idea, but don't hold me to it….

To estimate, fees for commercials, these days, are currently around $2,000 to $10,000, though this varies greatly by format, client, geographical region, and the experience level of the writer. There are some Internet companies that spin out short projects for much less, say $500 or so; the quality is often commensurate with the price. In the beginning of your career, you might do projects that don't pay well, just to build your portfolio. When you become well known, you'll get a lot more for writing film scores. But most projects for most writers fall in this general range of $2,000 to $10,000. That must cover everything involved in creating the recording, including studio fees, paying for live musicians, and so on.

NEGOTIATING PAYMENT

Negotiating payment involves discussing the project with the client and agreeing to a fee. The client may have a budget for the project, which would determine the maximum fee and production costs, but is willing to consider your thoughts about how best to accomplish the project and what the potential costs would be.

There are several ways that writer/producers structure payment.

- **Set rate.** Sometimes, the client will tell you that they are working within a limited budget and have a certain amount to spend on music. In this case, there is usually very little room for negotiations; it's a "take it or leave it" offer. The risk is that other writers may be pleased to do the job for the money that is offered.
- **Working on spec.** Working on speculation, or "spec," means you work for free, and you get paid only if your client sells their product. My first inclination is to say "no" to these kinds of projects, unless you really feel that this particular job could enhance your career. Be sure that you keep all copyrights for any work that you do on spec.
- **Residuals.** As mentioned earlier, some projects, particularly commercials, may pay *residuals*—money paid on a recurring basis for reuse of the same music. For example, commercials run in thirteen-week cycles, and there are four cycles per year. If the commercial is a success and runs for another cycle, in a residual deal the composer will get paid an additional 50 percent (the union rate). In this way, a single project can continue to pay you dividends for a long time after the work is done.
- **Royalty based.** Receiving royalties for your work—a percentage of the earned income (points)—can affect your initial fee. If you are writing and producing an album, you have the opportunity to make money every time the song is played on radio, television, or satellite, a CD or cassette of it is sold, if it appears on film, and when it is performed live. For these reasons, you may opt to work on a record in which you are the composer/producer for little money upfront (advance) with the hope that you will earn a continuous income from royalties if the record succeeds. (Read more about copyrights and royalties on pages 47–50.)

BUDGETING FOR JOBS

When you determine the budget or costs for a job, consider the following potential expenses:

Musicians' Contract Payments	Leader
	Contractor
	Orchestrator
	Arranger
	Copyist
	Sidemen
	P&W (pension and welfare)
	H&W (health and welfare)
	Payroll taxes (federal income tax, state income tax, social security, etc.)
Singers' Contract Payment	Vocalists
	Contractor (three or more; must be part of group)
	P&W (pension and welfare)
	Payroll taxes
Additional Costs	Recording studio
	Hourly charge (or daily charge)
	Outboard-gear rental
	Video lockup
	Materials (tape, CDs, DATs, etc.)
	Sales tax
	Engineer (freelance?)
Instrument Rental	Usually synths and percussion; also extra keyboards such as a Hammond B3 organ, etc.
Cartage	For large items: synth rigs, drums, guitar setup, percussion, acoustic bass, electric bass setup, harp, etc.
Payroll-Service Handling	Pays musician and singer session fees and payroll taxes; charge is usually 5–8 percent of musician/singer payments
Food/Refreshment	For clients on session
Shipping	Expedited or local
Legal	Write or review contract
Agent	5- to 20-percent fee

Miscellaneous	Temp help (typing, accounting, etc.)
	Phone calls
	Entertainment of clients (lunch)
	Travel costs (gas, parking, etc.)
	Accountant (IRS, state forms/filings)
	Other

When determining your costs, be sure to budget for studio time. An important consideration is whether or not you can professionally record and engineer with your own studio. If you have enough experience and feel competent, this is the best choice financially and timewise. However, if you are not equipped or experienced in recording live instruments, hiring an outside studio and/or professional engineer may be your best option. Hiring a pro frees up your time for production considerations (and often, for attending to clients) and can also be the cheapest and best engineering lesson you can get.

Your budget may permit the use of a large studio (which is always good for "corporate appearances"), but if you can obtain a good sound by setting up a microphone in the bathroom to record the vocals over your sequenced tracks, why not? A real bass might add a lot more to the feel, but as an underscore to a radio commercial with voiceover from top to bottom, how necessary is it? Is it really worth the extra expense to hire these musicians? These are just a few of the many decisions you will make in determining costs and production approaches.

Unexpected expenses can add up, so calculate each of these on a project-by-project basis. Remember to account for them in your next project budget. (Read more about booking outside studios on page 110.)

CREATING CONTRACTS

Create a contract for any job you are hired to do. If needed, you can hire a lawyer to create a basic contract that can be used repeatedly, though often, clients prefer using their own contracts. Contracts help you and your client understand what is expected of each other and ensure that there are no vague areas in a financial arrangement before a job has begun. Verbal agreements can lead to misunderstandings and, hence, many serious consequences. Even if the contract is for a small amount of money, put it in writing. If your client doesn't agree to a written agreement, beware. Strongly consider not accepting the job.

PROJECT 4.1. UNDERSTANDING CONTRACTS

Are you ready to sign a contract? Answer these questions.

1. How long does it usually take you to prepare music? Try to ballpark an amount based on time and the number of instruments. Include time spent writing and mixing, and also for administrative tasks such as coordinating musicians and sending invoices.

2. How much does it cost you to do a project, in terms of time and necessary expenses? Are there expenses you know that you must incur, such as for studio time or equipment rental?

3. What is the minimum rate you are willing to work for? Note that you should try to negotiate for an amount that is above your minimum. What is a realistic, preferred rate? Use your findings from the first two steps to inform this decision, as well as your research of the rates in your geographical region and genre.

4. What language should you insist be present or absent in a contract? Find a contract to use as a model, preferably from someone who works in your region, in the same industry, and customize it. Though you will nearly always be given a contract by a client, you should be ready to send someone your own contract if they request that you draft one.

5. Prepare a template for your invoice. At the bottom, write "Payable within thirty days."

6. What's your plan for when a client doesn't pay? Industry practice is to give them thirty days, and then automatically follow up with a second invoice and telephone call, asking for immediate payment. If you haven't received it within two weeks, you can send a third demand, with the additional note that if they don't pay within two weeks, you'll be forced to defer the case to a collection agency. This is a last resort for you, as it will end your relationship with

the client, and the agency will get about 50 percent of the payment due to you. Try to resolve the situation amicably first. But have your plan ready, just in case.

GETTING AND PROTECTING YOUR COPYRIGHTS

If you write songs, one of the most important legal matters you may encounter in your professional life is copyright law. Copyright is your legal protection for a piece of intellectual property that you have created and chronicled by mechanical or graphic means (i.e., your recordings and songs).

Every work that is published in the United States is subject to mandatory deposit with the Library of Congress. The 1976 Copyright Act defines music publication as follows:

Publication is the distribution of copies of phonorecords of a work to the public by sale or other transfer of ownership, or by rental, lease, or lending. The offering to distribute copies of phonorecords to a group of persons for purposes of further distribution, public performance, or public display constitutes publication. A public performance or display of a work does not of itself constitute publication.

A musical work is deemed to be published when it has been recorded and/or printed and gone into public distribution. A musical work is *not* considered to be published if the "material object," or the tangible copy, does not change hands or is not offered for sale to the public. This could include a television performance of a work that has not been recorded.

Copyright law does not protect you if you have created the lyrics for a song and related them to a colleague without having written them down. If you improvised a lyric to a song in a jam session but didn't write the lyrics down or record them, you do not own the copyright. *You are deemed to have copyright the moment you finish writing the lead sheet or finish recording the song.*

Musical creations that are not copyrightable include song titles, most short musical phrases, drum grooves, and generic rhythm parts. Other creations that are in the public domain and/or contain no original authorship are not copyrightable, such as folk songs.

As the copyright owner, you own all of the rights in regards to the copying and distribution of your music. This can be an important income source. When you copyright a work, you have the right to reproduce, prepare derivative works, distribute copies or recordings, perform the work in public, and broadcast the work publicly by means of digital audio transmission, in any way you deem appropriate. You also have the right to authorize others to do these things. You can let people use your work for free, for a licensing fee, for a one-time cash payment, etc. It is your property to do with as you wish.

REGISTERING YOUR COPYRIGHTS

There are two types of registerable musical works: a **musical composition** and a **sound recording**. Copyright law states that the copyright for a musical composition goes to the author(s), i.e. the composer and lyricist. The music can be in the form of a lead sheet or a recording. However, submitting a recording of your music does not constitute your copyright of the sound recording. The copyright for a *sound recording* of the song will generally go to the performer, record company, or producer, even though the composer still retains copyright for the song itself.

United States copyright law requires that two copies of every published work be registered with the Library of Congress within three months of the work's inception. Register your work with the Library of Congress Copyright Office by obtaining and filing a Form PA for performing arts or a Form SR for sound recordings. If the song is unpublished, you must submit one copy on a record, tape, or lead sheet (or if it is published, two copies), along with a $30 registration fee. You can download the forms and learn more about copyrights on the Library of Congress's Web site.

If for any reason you are going to court for copyright infringement, the registration of your work can have a strong impact on the final outcome. It is certainly evidence of time of creation and can affect damages that are awarded.

For works that are not registered anonymously or under a pseudonym, and are not works done for hire (as a matter of employment), the copyright is valid for seventy years after the death of the composer, or in the case of several writers, the death of the last surviving writer. After the death of the writer, the writer's estate maintains the copyright.

INDUSTRY SPOTLIGHT: WORK FOR HIRE

"Work for hire" is a special category of copyright law. It applies to any music you write as an employee, as part of your employment responsibilities. It also applies to work you do if hired as a contractor by an independent firm, such as an advertising agency, computer-game developer, or film company, to write music for a specific application. For the purposes of copyright in work-for-hire situations, the employer, or the person that hired you as an individual contractor (with a written agreement, entered into expressly agreeing that this was a work for hire), owns the copyright and is considered to be the writer. The copyright for works for hire last for ninety-five years after publication or one-hundred-twenty years from the date of creation, whichever is the shortest.

For example, if you are an employee of a videogame company and you compose the theme music, you own none of the creative rights (in this case, the copyright) for this creation; the corporation does, unless you have negotiated otherwise. Other "work-for-hire" copyright examples include: jingles composed and/or arranged within the scope of an employee relationship for a jingle firm, and sound recordings by staff engineers. As the writer, you can only maintain your rights of authorship and copyright with the express written agreement by employer, who thereby relinquishes their copyright and authorship.

In November 1999, the U. S. Congress passed an amendment to the Copyright Act of 1976 that has caused outrage among recording artists who are contracted to record labels. Prior to this amendment, the sound recording (SR) copyright belonged to the record label for a period of thirty-five years, after which time the ownership of the master recordings reverted to the artists. This new amendment now deems any sound recording done for a record label as a "work for hire," and hence the copyright for that recording could hypothetically remain with the label in perpetuity.

ROYALTIES: GETTING YOUR SHARE

The funds you earn from your copyrighted works are called royalties. Royalties for any piece of music are divided in two. Half is the writer's share; half is the publisher's share. (By "publisher," we are not referring to a company that prints sheet music. In this context, the publisher is the entity that owns and manages the licensing, synchronization, or mechanical reproduction rights to a song.) For example, if a song earns $1,000,000, the writer's share is $500,000 and the publisher's share is $500,000. This is why you have to be very vigilant and use a lawyer when publishing is negotiated. The very first thing a record company or client may want to do is get the publishing share. (Be very cautious about giving up your writer's share.)

The writer's share may also be further divided into two halves, between the music composers and the lyricists. The percentages should be formally agreed to beforehand by the writers/authors. If there are no lyrics, the composer gets 100 percent. To put this in real terms, if that $500,000 above is divided equally among three composers and one lyricist, the composers would get about $83,333 each, while the lyricist would get $250,000. The publisher would still get $500,000.

To get an idea of how these agreements manifest themselves, look on the liner notes of any given record. You will see that many times, there are several publishers and several composers. If you are associated with a hit record, the financial gain can easily reach millions of dollars, of which the publisher is paid a large sum. This is one example demonstrating how critical it is to get an experienced entertainment lawyer to negotiate on your behalf.

DOUBLE YOUR MONEY: BECOME YOUR OWN PUBLISHER

Let's look again at the royalty distribution. The writer makes 50 percent, and the publisher makes 50 percent. So what if you became your own publisher? Another 50 percent. Looks pretty good, doesn't it?

However, there is work involved. The music publisher owns the rights to a song, but that ownership role, although it seems to be token at first, is very important. The publisher of the music administers the business end. This includes arranging and negotiating where, when, and by whom the music will be used—and for how much. The publisher has three primary roles: (1) to market and promote the copyrighted songs in its catalog, (2) to manage the copyrights and administer and collect funds earned by the songs, and (3) to protect the songwriter from copyright infringements. And, if you're the writer/publisher, your role is also to keep filling the publishing house's (that is, *your*) song coffers.

An example of the power of the publisher involves the situation of Michael Jackson purchasing the publishing rights for all of the Beatles music from Paul McCartney. Michael Jackson was able to negotiate hefty sums of money for the use of this very familiar music in jingles and television shows. As a result, Michael Jackson, Paul McCartney, and the estate of John Lennon will share in all of the royalties, licensing fees, synchronization fees, etc. that this music generates.

PROTECTING YOUR RIGHTS: PERFORMANCE RIGHTS ORGANIZATIONS (PROS)

When you compose a piece of music, it is your intellectual property and it immediately takes on an unquantified value. The financial value of your work is determined by the demand for its use. As the writer, you cannot go door to door in the world and collect a few cents from everyone who buys or uses your music. That is the role of the performance rights organization.

A performance rights organization (PRO) is a nonprofit organization that sells licenses, granting permission to use copyrighted music to organizations such as radio and television stations, film companies, bars, restaurants, jingle houses, airlines, Internet sites, or even orchestras. These groups use copyrighted music in exchange for a licensing fee. The licensing fee is collected by the PRO and subsequently distributed to the copyright holder (that's you).

There are three PROs recognized by the U.S. Copyright Act: the Society of European Stage Authors and Composers (SESAC), American Society of Composers, Authors, and Publishers (ASCAP), and Broadcast Music Incorporated (BMI). At one time, each of these PROs had specific areas of music that it focused on. For example, SESAC, founded in 1930, was limited to European and gospel music. ASCAP, founded in 1914, is the oldest performance rights organization. Originally, it dealt with the popular music of the day, representing composers such as Irving Berlin, Richard Rodgers, Harold Arlen, and Jerome Kern. BMI, founded in 1940 to represent writers—many of whom were not eligible to join the other two PROs under membership guidelines—focused primarily on blues, country, jazz, r&b, and Spanish language. Nowadays, all three PROs cross over into all styles of music. BMI is the largest and SESAC is the smallest.

It is crucial that you join a performance rights organization (PRO) as a writer, and also as a publisher as soon as you anticipate that your music will become recorded and/or will be performed live. You must do this in order to collect your fair share of royalties for radio and television airplay, mechanical royalties, synchronization fees, live performance, use of your music by other artists, performances on the Internet, and other outlets.

In respect to the licensing of your music, if you are (a) a signatory publisher with a PRO, and (b) you still own all of the publishing associated with your composition, then the PRO can still collect your negotiated licensing fee on your behalf by having the client submit payment to the PRO. As the publisher of your own music, you can also agree to the licensing of your music and collect your fee independent of a PRO. If another entity holds the publishing to your music and/or acts as an agent for the licensing of your music, then the PRO will probably not be involved in this transaction.

Your research will help you determine which PRO is best for you. There is no application fee, but there might be a small annual administration fee for both composer and publisher. Choose carefully; each PRO surveys and tracks usage and play of copyrighted music in its own manner. Investigate before joining. Learn as much as you can about each organization and see which one is the best fit for what you are doing.

Two other important organizations to be aware of, particularly in the fields of television, commercial, and film music, are the National Music Publisher's Association (NMPA) and the Harry Fox Agency (HFA).

- **National Music Publisher's Association (NMPA).** The National Music Publisher's Association was formed in 1917 to represent music publishers primarily in the fields of copyright legislation and protection. It was instrumental in representing publishers in the Copyright Act of 1976 and continues to lobby on the publisher's behalf as the technology of recorded music changes rapidly.
- **Harry Fox Agency (HFA).** The Harry Fox Agency, Inc. was formed in 1927 by the NMPA to provide a monitoring and negotiating service and information source for licensing musical copyrights. HFA is distinct from the PROs in that it represents solely music publishers and not writers. It now has more than 23,000 publisher affiliates. As a writer who

also owns the publishing rights to your music, you could join ASCAP, BMI, or SESAC, and as publisher you could join HFA. The PRO would represent you in the collection of your share of composer's royalties, while HFA would represent the publishing half of your copyrighted music.

Performance Rights Organization Contact Info

ASCAP
ASCAP Building
One Lincoln Plaza
New York, NY 10023
1-800-95-ASCAP
www.ascap.com

BMI
320 West 57th Street
New York, NY 10019-3790
212-586-2000
www.bmi.com

Harry Fox Agency (HFA)
711 3rd Avenue
New York, NY 10017
212-370-5330

National Music Publisher's Association (NMPA)
475 Park Avenue South, 29th Floor
New York, NY 10016-6901
646-742-1651

SESAC
55 Music Square East
Nashville, TN 37203
615-320-0055

When you join a PRO as a publisher and/or composer, that PRO will represent your right to be paid for having your copyrighted music played in public. The PROs monitor how much your music is played by the use of broadcast logs for radio and television, television and film cue sheets, trade magazines and chart activity, census surveys, reports of live performances from you, computer database information, and so on to calculate your share of the pie. Based on certain formulas, the PRO sends a check to both the writer and the publisher, based on the performance information they have collected.

This right is strictly enforced by U.S. copyright law, which states that any entity playing or performing copyrighted music is legally obligated to secure permission to present this music, whether it is recorded (mechanical) or live. The music user does this by paying this licensing fee to the three PROs in the United States. For some large radio stations, record companies, and television stations, these licensing fees can cost from hundreds of thousands to millions of dollars. Failure to pay these fees is an infringement of copyright law.

Through these fees, the PROs accumulate billions of dollars annually. This revenue goes into large funds that are distributed according to how much any given piece of music is played proportionally to the others in the same PRO. Hence, a number 1 *Billboard* hit can bring the writers millions of dollars. One writer I knew had a song reach number 1 on both the pop and country charts, and he received a first royalty check of $1,000,000.

The PROs will usually divide the fees collected according to the venue in which the copyrighted music is performed. For example, all licensing fees collected from radio stations are divided among those composers whose music is played on the radio. All fees collected from concert halls are divided among the composers whose works are performed in those concert halls. This provides for a fair and equitable division of specific licensing fees.

Another critical function that the PROs perform is the licensing of music for film and television. The amount of the fee is determined by an agreement between the film's producers and the song's publisher(s), and relies on a number of factors. When the agreement is set, the PRO can track the theater and television performances, radio and television promotion and airplay, and sales of soundtrack albums, and distribute the monies for airplay and mechanical royalties appropriately.

The three PROs now allow access to your accounts via their Web sites. You can track your financial status there and anticipate what your income will be.

The business of copyright, publishing, and licensing may be fundamental to your success. Without an understanding of these elements, it is very possible that you can lose income to which you are entitled. I should know; it happened to me on several occasions early in my career. So be diligent and informed when dealing in the business world. Let your clients know that you understand this part of the business and expect to be treated fairly and honestly.

PROJECT 4.2. PROTECTING YOUR COPYRIGHTS

1. What is your PRO? If you don't have one, immediately register.
2. Are you ready to register a copyright? Do you have all the forms or Web links on hand? If not, get that all in place, so

that you can register a new copyright quicky and efficiently, should the need arise. If you've never done it before, go through the process on one of your compositions.

CONCLUSION

For many freelancers (in all fields), getting paid is among the most difficult aspects of running the business. Advance preparation for all these administrative tasks will help you complete the billing process more effectively. Be sure to include an invoice with your final delivery, and write "Payable within thirty days of receipt" at the bottom. Mark this date on your calendar, and if your payment is not received by then, immediately and politely follow up with both another written invoice and a phone call. Have a plan in place for when a client doesn't deliver promptly after a second notice. Hopefully, the need will never arise, but if you require the services of a collection agency, it's helpful to have one in place before the time comes in which they are needed. At that point, you may be in a cash-flow bind, and will need as prompt a resolution as possible.

CHAPTER **5**
Being Your Own Producer

Ready for another whiteboard message?

Students often look inwardly, at standards, to determine whether their work is good or not. In school, their standard is how good their music is in relationship to their classmates' music.

Once they graduate, their standard suddenly must change. If they are film writers, the standard goes from Bob in the dorm to Howard Shore, John Williams, and Danny Elfman. For jingle writers, the standard becomes Don Sebesky and Crushing Music.

As a writer, you can't be less than that. That's where your competition is, and your standards must be up there before you start writing professionally. It's what your clients expect from you.

Standards for jingles and such are the same as for albums. Commercial music looks to albums, as their standards, and to see what styles of music people listen to. Keep track of what's on the *Billboard* charts, and make sure that you can recreate those sounds.

Writers frequently bring me their recordings. One singer/songwriter dropped by, recently, and asked me what I thought. His music had an acoustic folk sound, a bit like James Taylor.

So, I put his CD in one player, and a James Taylor CD in another one, and we listened to them side by side. You might guess that James Taylor's music was a couple notches up.

In the beginning, it's painful to look at this, but it's also extremely important. In the record store, the buyer's standard will be James Taylor. Yours must be too, if you are competing for the same listeners.

My standard is the highest professional standard I can accomplish, and that's what I expect from my students (at least, from the ones in their fourth year, about to graduate). It's what clients expect from you! I want you to be really good. I want you to have the highest standard. And so does your client.

To work in the world of the professionals, you need to think of yourself as being up there, and then figure out how to get to that level, if you're not already there.

The great writers I've worked with work twenty-four hours a day. As soon as a show is over, they're back at the hotel, writing. They are always bringing in new material, and revising their old work.

Furthermore, don't settle for a mediocre mix. Informed clients know the difference. A client might say it's good for a student project, but they won't pay you a hundred grand a year to write for them.

When you're wearing your Producer's hat, maintaining standards is part of your job. It can be difficult, though, because as creative artists, we writers get so far inside our work, and producers must be objective. And this quality standard isn't just about the quality of the recording or the composition: it's how well the piece suits the client's needs.

It's a dilemma. Whether we're writing a love song on an album or an underscore for a dog food commercial, you're working with a duality of functions. As an artist, there's always a personal relationship between you and your music. On the other hand, you're creating a product for a purpose. It's hard to do both at the same time, and modern writer/producers have a bigger job than our predecessors in decades past did, when different people fulfilled these responsibilities.

It comes down to the business being priority. To achieve a successful commercial composition, we must remove any emotional attachment to the music, knowing that it's a product. The businessperson, wearing the "P" hat, must ensure that the music serves its contracted function.

One fights this duality, from time to time. We might like a form or structure musically, even though it doesn't serve the client's purpose. For example, you might have an extra verse that serves the song's narrative really well, lyrically, but the song is too long. Objectivity is often difficult, but paramount.

To be a good advocate for your client, you need to detach yourself from the music and deliver a final product that conforms to what your client needs. There are many steps that can make this process easier, in the long run. This chapter prepares you for some of the production-specific issues that may arise during recording.

PRODUCING THE "PERFECT" TRACK

What is a perfect track? It can be any number of things, but one thing is certain: it is something different for everyone. In my opinion, a perfect track is one that makes the client or listener say, "I love it." Whether or not it's to your own personal taste is irrelevant. It's whether you've satisfied your client's needs.

The digital and MIDI revolution can provide technical perfection. Music can be in perfect time. Auto-tune programs digitally correct tuning, so most intonation problems have become a thing of the past. A singer has only to sing one great line in a chorus and it can be digitally repeated, modulated, inverted, or harmonized to make a "perfect" performance. But would the result be a perfect track?

The perfection of any art can only be measured subjectively by its impact on the human spirit and the purpose it serves. Many consider Neil Young to be the perfect singer. How about Bob Dylan? Are they any more "perfect" than Luciano Pavarotti? Producing live recorded performances is, in essence, no different than it has ever been. What you are trying to do is capture the "magic"—that unknown quality that comes from great musicians creating fine music. By setting your standards at the highest level of production, you will recognize when everything is right. It is one of the mystical elements of recording live music: it can happen at any time, or not at all.

The first step in achieving these "perfect" tracks is in the composition. The writing must be strong and fulfill its purpose. If your writing does not fulfill the intentions you set out to achieve, the whole production suffers. But composition alone is not enough. The production and the performances bring the composition to life.

As the producer, you will be looking for the essential elements from the performers, such as correct notes, a strong groove or feel, good sound, captivating delivery of the melody, effective musical communication, and a sense of "magic." Magic is the term that I use to describe times when the production works so well that the music takes on a new life beyond what you had expected. It can be that special moment that you created in the writing, a magnificent and inspired performance from the musicians, or an amazing mix that breathes life into the track. On the spur of the moment, you might come up with a recording, miking, or mixing approach that contributes something special. Weigh the benefits of these ideas by how they enhance the music versus the additional financial and time commitment.

During the session, don't let the tiniest mistake go by if you have the time to correct it. Don't allow yourself to think, "No one is going to notice this small musical flaw." Pay attention to every detail, as each one adds to the greatness of the whole.

Another element of a "perfect" track is the way it sounds. Know the sound quality you want to achieve, so you can judge the final product fairly. As writers, we have to be aware of how our music stands up to the standard of professionalism and quality that exists in the marketplace. If your goal is to write commercial hit songs, listen to the radio, watch MTV, VH1, and MuchMusic, and buy plenty of recordings. If you want to write for film or television, listen closely to the scores of films or television shows. Pay particular attention to advertising jingles and station IDs, as well. There is a lot of great music being produced out there and you have to live up to those standards. Whether or not you like a particular song or track is irrelevant. The point is to study and appreciate the *quality* and *integrity* that exists at that level.

Listening to and analyzing "perfect" music is the best way to develop "perfect" hearing. Each recording is a jigsaw puzzle containing thousands of pieces that have to be organized and assembled. As the producer, you have to "fit" each detail together to craft a perfect piece of recorded music.

ENSURING PERFECT TRACKS THROUGH PEOPLE SKILLS

You increase your chances of getting the perfect track if you manage the recording session well. As the producer, *you* are responsible for the finished product. Sometimes it may seem that every person involved in the recording has a unique agenda, which can affect the project and its outcome. As a producer, you will have to make tough decisions quickly and decisively and need to be a master of public relations and clear communication, so that everyone on the project remains productive. When I finally understood that it was important to put my client first and maintain high production values, I crossed an important bridge to production peace of mind and sanity. Over time, you will find the ways that work best for you, but there are some basic steps that will make your productions go smoothly and be as stress free as possible.

- **Hire the best musicians available.** That is production rule number 1. Great studio musicians make your work seem effortless. There are players who have a particular sound or who are masters of particular styles, singers who brilliantly interpret melodies, musicians known for their versatility or impeccable intonation, excellent soloists, skilled ensemble contributors, musicians who can read, and musicians who can't. Get to know the good music contractors in your town, because their job is to *know* the best musicians. They can do a lot of the legwork for you.

- **Know what you want ahead of time and accept the fact that you might not get *exactly* what you wanted.** Before you start recording, ask yourself, "What is the focus and objective of my production?" That way you won't waste time going in the wrong direction. The extra forty-five minutes used during tracking may very well cut into mixing time; hence, that second guitar part may have to be forsaken. Learn to formulate contingency plans quickly by considering possible alternatives before starting the recording.

  Deadlines often force you to make decisions on the fly. This is where the art of production improvisation is developed and comes into play. You have to make decisions quietly and calmly, and appear to be in command of the situation all of the time. A musical disaster can often go unnoticed by your client, so the *last* thing that you want to do is to make them aware of any difficulties. If you behave like a leader, you *are* a leader, especially during unplanned situations.

- **Keep the session moving and limit social discussions to before and after the session.** When the "meter" starts

running, get right down to business and save the pleasant-
ries until after the session. Virtually everyone involved in
the production process is doing this for their living and will
expect to be paid for the time they invest, which includes
social time.

- **Develop great studio skills and a solid knowledge of technology.** Take the time to fully understand how to record your
music in a productive and meaningful way, and to speak
the "language of recording" to musicians and engineers.
Some of the greatest producers in history had limited or no
engineering background at all. George Martin, the father
of modern production and producer of virtually all of the
Beatles' music, was not an engineer. However, he did have a
solid knowledge of the recording environment and understood how to get the most out of the available technology.
Other great producers, such as Quincy Jones, Phil Spector,
Russ Titleman, Jack Richardson, L.A. and Babyface, Jam and
Lewis, David Foster, Walter Afanasieff, and John Leventhal,
come from writing backgrounds—but you can be sure that
they understand studio technology.

- **Develop peripheral hearing.** Just as peripheral vision is the
ability to see images out of our main line of sight, peripheral hearing is the ability to recognize mistakes and musical
anomalies while listening to another musical focal point.
There could be a wrong chord, a missed drum fill, or any
other mistake, big or small. By training your ears to become
used to perfection as the norm, even the smallest mistake in
a track will become evident immediately. If you are unsure
about what you heard, take the few minutes to check.

- **Write playable music.** At the risk of overstating the obvious,
it is important that you write music that is playable. It is
almost impossible to have a successful production if the
music is unplayable, because you will spend most of your
time converting your unplayable passages into playable ones.
If you have well-written charts with the right orchestrational
ranges and concepts, the musicians/artists will play these to
perfection.

- **Speak your client's language.** Most of the time, the clients
will know what they want, but may not be able to express
their thoughts in musical terms. You will hear a variety of

interesting descriptions. Some may say, "Make the music more *sizzly/jangly/arrogant/brown*," or "Have the voiceover artist put more emphasis on a particular word or on the third syllable of the word." Through experience, you will become an excellent translator of "clientese" into the more familiar "musician-speak." It will make your productions run smoothly and effortlessly.

PREPARING FOR THE RECORDING SESSION

Much of your success in the studio will depend on your preparation. Before you commence recording, firmly establish the following:

- ✔ Is your client able to reach you at any time, and can you reach your client?
- ✔ In what format will you be recording?
- ✔ Where will you be recording?
- ✔ Have you allowed enough time to comfortably complete the project?
- ✔ If you are using MIDI-based tracks with live-musician overdubs, are the tracks absolutely perfect and all of the synchronization preparation completed?
- ✔ Do you/they have adequate computer hard drive space, external disk drives, or CDs to store your music?
- ✔ How many musicians will be involved and have they all been contacted and confirmed for the session?
- ✔ If you are using live players, are you prepared with a professional score and parts?
- ✔ Have you, the music contractors, or talent agencies completed the necessary contracts for the players and artists? (This frequently happens after the recording session.)
- ✔ What are your contractual responsibilities and have you chosen the most efficient way to fulfill them?
- ✔ Have you left enough contingency time for any last-minute emergencies and technical glitches? Something unexpected always occurs.
- ✔ Have you provided for catering, snacks, and other amenities for a long session?
- ✔ Do you have your contact list in case someone cancels at the last minute or just doesn't show up?

✔ Who, other than the talent, will be present at the session(s), and have you provided for their comfort?

Before each recording session, prioritize your goals to ensure that you complete everything that must be done. When budgeting for studio time, include time for setup and recording, and establish the minimum recording requirements. Many things can happen during the course of a recording session that will require you to make immediate decisions regarding the nature of the recording. You need to know what to do next. Be adamant and professional about keeping the session running smoothly and efficiently.

I recall working for a writer/producer as the session bassist on a series of orchestral pop albums. The writer/producer had worked long and hard on completing a few pieces in addition to those he was hired to record for the albums, and hoped to squeeze them into his budgeted recording time. He was excited to have a full orchestra available to record *all* of his music. However, on the first day, the session fell into shambles due to a synchronization glitch between the multitrack and his computer-generated tracks. There were more than fifty musicians getting paid to wait while the engineer and writer/producer tried to solve the problem. After what seemed like an eternity—particularly to the impatient client, who was furious that his money was "going down the tubes"—the system was *kind of* working. This is where the writer/producer had to prioritize. The extra music he had poured his heart and soul into had to be left behind, while we recorded the music that he had been hired to produce. We barely had enough time in the three days to complete the songs for the albums, and his other tunes were never recorded.

Often, you will go into the studio with ambitious plans, but will find that time becomes limited and you'll have to decide which of the elements of the composition are most important and which can be forsaken. For example, if a vocal is the focal point of your track, spend the time (if you have it) perfecting that track, rather than taking the time to go back and punch in instrumental corrections that could also be "fixed in the mix." Stating in a firm but gentle manner, "We're moving on," is very decisive and effective. Studio musicians, who are being paid to be there, will understand and object only if there are gross problems in their performances.

If you had imagined a doubled guitar track, a hi-hat overdub, a doubled string section, and a Hammond B3 organ overdub, but run the risk of not completing your session, wait to see if there is time at the end of the session to add these extras. Many times during the recording, a new idea will come to you. Don't let this rule your session. Similarly, try not to be swayed by the musicians' or engineers' suggestions, no matter how great they are, if they are going to pose a threat to the completion of your recording.

A dreaded word in the commercial field, mainly from the production end, is "overtime." Overtime usually involves extra payments beyond the initial budget, which will most likely come out of *your* pocket. Pad your budget slightly to allow for such occurrences. However, anything longer than a half hour of overtime usually is your personal "donation."

On rare occasions, you won't be able to finish a session. This is incredibly stressful and can be damaging to your career if you don't handle it in the right way. If a session is going poorly, you will have to make some tough decisions. I have seen musicians let go during sessions, producers complaining to studio managers because of engineering incompetence or equipment failure, musicians and singers losing their patience because they don't have a good headphone mix, and clients who have become unhappy with the recording while it is still in session. You will have to develop creative ways to work around problems. I have done everything from recording vocals in my bathroom at 3 A.M. to playing improvised bass solos with the machine at half speed in order to "duplicate" a guitar solo when played at normal speed, because the guitar player didn't show up.

In the freelance writing/producing field, most deadlines are unyielding. If you are writing for television, the music will usually be the last element to be added. You don't want to be the one who holds up the final version of a show that will be aired in a week or two. You will have to be resolute and organized, and can't leave things to the last minute.

MAINTAINING CONTROL AS THE PRODUCER

It is said that the strength of a relationship isn't measured by how things are in the good times, but how they survive during the rough times. In commercial music production, the writer/producer is the captain of the entire crew, whose collective efforts contribute to the final product.

Sometimes, even the best producer has to rescue the sinking ship. Perhaps the musicians show up late or incapacitated—or don't show up at all. The copyist may have copied parts incorrectly, and you must make corrections during the session. Or, the client may be unhappy with the musicians' performances. Worse, you may find that the engineer is having technical problems in the studio, while your whole cast of musicians waits. I have witnessed all of these things countless times. Most of the time, producers do what they have to do: stay calm, isolate the problem, and rectify it. A producer who is nervous will find that this anxiety can easily filter through to the artists, the engineer, assistant engineer, studio manager, and tech staff.

The producer sets the tone of the recording sessions. If you are positive and encouraging, your session will reflect this. Similarly, if you fall into the depths of despair over a bad moment, your recording will follow suit very quickly. For this reason, you must stay focused and be the driving force behind getting the job done. You must "take care of business" in a professional and timely manner.

What do you do when the session is rolling and the client is not happy? There is no point in getting mad. Instead, take a diplomatic tack. Figure out what the client wants and how you can best provide it. Ask for the client's opinions, starting your questions with, "How do you think. . . ." This will initiate a healthy dialog. Remember that you both have something in common: a desire to fix the problem as quickly as possible.

PROJECT 5.1. EVALUATE YOUR SKILLS

List your strengths and weaknesses as a writer/producer/engineer. Where do you most need to improve: In your technical knowledge of writing? Of sound engineering? Quality of your gear/studio? People skills? Experience? How will these improve? Don't get a complex about this, as everyone starts from somewhere. Just recognize where you need to grow, and create a plan to improve.

CONCLUSION

As your own producer, you must take responsibility for the quality standard of the product. The final outcome will depend on the quality of your skills, your gear, your ability to listen to your client, and your ability to communicate with musicians. Understand your personal strengths and weaknesses in these areas, and work to bring all aspects of your abilities to the highest quality standard.

CHAPTER 6

Working with Musicians

THE CHOICE OF INSTRUMENTALISTS, SINGERS, AND ARTISTS is one of the most critical elements of production, since that determines the sound of your final product. How do you determine who to hire? From a purely business perspective, you want the person who will do the best job for the money you have to spend. This doesn't always mean the least-expensive person. Each musician will bring something unique to the creative experience—a distinctive sound, musical approach, or overall ability to work and cooperate in the studio environment.

Always use performers who have an excellent reputation and with whom you are comfortable. The performers must be team players who are interested in pleasing the producer, will add musicianship to the overall sound, and can get the job done.

If you have only one hour to complete a jingle session, you will generally need people who can read well. These musicians might not be the best players for the style you have written, but they will probably get the job done quickly. A great reader is someone who can, at sight, read the music while recording a track and make it sound like they have played it a thousand times. These musicians are the most *cost-effective* players for sessions with a time constraint.

A common mistake my production students make is in being too shy about approaching the best performers. Often, though, the best players are in the same circumstance, and trying to find good writer/producers with whom to collaborate. Just ask them. They might be interested. If they are too busy, they might know another good player who might be available.

The choice of a vocalist is usually more important than the choice of an instrumentalist. The singer that appears to be breathtaking in live performance may not necessarily transmit that magic into the recording studio. Small intonation and timing problems that go by unnoticed on stage will become immediately evident when you are recording. All of the magic of the performance has to be conveyed solely through the recorded medium without the visual impact and spontaneity of a live performance. In choosing vocalists, ensure that you are familiar with their stylistic strengths, vocal range, vocal timbre, attitude, abilities within a particular genre, and, if necessary, their ability to sing in a vocal background group.

Also pay particular attention to the drummer you choose. The drummer is the cornerstone of the feel. Successful freelance studio drummers have their roots in r&b, rock, country, and funk, or have mastered these genres, but be sure to know stylistic strengths in advance. These musicians are usually great at playing simple grooves, playing with a click track, and supporting the music. Most successful studio drummers have great-sounding kits.

PREPARING FOR LIVE MUSICIANS AT THE SESSION

A key part of your preparation is making sure that all of the contracted musicians and artists are booked and confirmed. Keep a list of the instrumentation you need, with corresponding phone numbers for several competent performers on each instrument. This will make the phone work a lot easier. Most professionals are easy to contact at any time. They will have pagers, cell phones, or answering services that forward messages. If you are using a contractor or agency, make sure you have a contact who is there to help you. A contractor's first commitment is to provide you with appropriate talent. They will do all that they can to make this part of the project go well.

When confirming with musicians, remind them of the type of gig it is, how long it will take, and how much and when they are going to get paid. Musicians, especially younger ones, are usually reluctant to ask how much they are getting paid, so tell them in advance. They will be happy to work with you as their career grows because they know you are upfront. If possible, pay your musicians right after the gig or even before they play. This leaves a good feeling with them, and even better, it is one less expense that you have to worry about later.

If you are using live musicians, it is imperative that you prepare for them. Get the performers in and out of the studio as quickly as possible, saving you time and money. Great players will do the job quickly if *you* are organized. Most importantly, create neat and accurate parts, and double-check them before the session starts. If you are disorganized, your session will be disorganized. In the microscopic environment of the studio, every issue seems to be magnified a thousand times.

Pre-Session Checklist—Live Musicians

○ Studio available, confirmed, and informed with details such as instrumentation, video lockup, etc.

○ Musicians confirmed.

○ AFM contract, other contracts, and necessary paperwork completed (often occurs after the session).

○ Alternate musicians' availability and numbers, should problems arise.

○ Notated music, as necessary.

○ Neat, legible parts that contain the correct amount of measures, are correctly transposed for appropriate instruments, and include all necessary markings— measure numbers, articulations, dynamics, phrasing, etc.

○ Extra copies of parts.

○ All cues (different pieces) labeled correctly, if applicable. Cues placed on the music stands in order of performance before session starts.

○ Extra copies of score for engineer and conductor (if needed).

○ Performers have a copy of the MIDI tracks and music beforehand, if desired.

○ Blank W2 forms for musicians to complete (needed for payment purposes).

Musician Confirmation Sheet

Name	Instrument	Phone Number(s)	Union Affiliation (if applicable)	Confirmed	Time Booked

WORKING WITH THE UNIONS

As a producer, you will probably have to deal directly with three unions at some point: the American Federation of Musicians (AFM), the Screen Actors Guild (SAG), and the American Federation of Television and Radio Artists (AFTRA).

- **American Federation of Musicians (AFM)** is a group of over 600 local branches representing professional musicians' interests in both the United States and Canada. The AFM is a union dedicated to all musicians (except vocalists), though not all musicians belong to a union. At the higher echelons of many aspects of performance, the musicians' union is strong and viable. The union is still involved in many jingle sessions, film sessions, symphony orchestras, theaters, albums, and television, particularly in the major music markets of New York, Los Angeles, Chicago, and Nashville.

- When your production company becomes larger and your clients become more high profile, it will be in your very best interest to become a signatory to the union, file union contracts, and hire union musicians. They are generally the best players in their respective fields and will do a great job. Your budget for the use of union musicians will include their pay, their pension, and the submission of work dues on their behalf.

- **Screen Actors Guild (SAG).** The Screen Actors Guild represents nearly 120,000 actors in film, television, and industrial, commercial, and music video. SAG is instrumental in improving actors' working conditions, compensation, and benefits. It is the premier labor union for actors and for vocalists on most television commercials.

- **American Federation of Television and Radio Artists (AFTRA)** represents actors, singers, announcers, and Foley (sound effects) artists. Similar to the AFM, it protects its members by first establishing working conditions, minimum pay standards (scale) for various types of work, and a system for the collection and distribution of session and residual payments. It also provides a pension plan, health and dental insurance plans, and other benefits.

AFTRA, SAG Artists

Finding non-AFTRA, non-SAG talent is a lot more difficult than finding those who will work for flat fees on a nonunion basis. There are several reasons:

1. Performers are more comfortable having their union collect their money and pension than chasing it down themselves.

2. Most professional actors who do voiceovers are represented by agencies that only deal with AFTRA or SAG members.

3. Singers (who can also be AFM members) will generally use AFTRA contracts, as the pay and residual formula is far superior to the AFM formula.

4. SAG and AFTRA members have to earn their way into the union through experience. Their annual dues are substantially higher than the AFM, which in turn means that SAG and AFTRA are able to benefit the membership on a more personal basis.

5. Scale for AFTRA and SAG talent is very high, and it is of no benefit for members to work nonunion contracts, as this means giving up many of their protections.

I am of the personal belief that all of our interests are best served by hiring AFM union musicians and AFTRA/SAG artists. They are generally the best artists available, and by supporting the union, you are helping to support the rights and future of all artists.

When you are working with contracted union musicians, file all of the necessary paperwork. Check with the union beforehand to determine what paperwork is needed. Some paperwork can't be completed until after the session. Have copies of the contracts with you during the session, just in case you need to refer to them. It is also a good idea to keep the union bylaws and pay-scale handbook in your briefcase, in case there are any questions from the players about pay, overtime, minimum contracted performance time, and amount of music to be recorded. If you are using a contractor to hire the musicians, make sure the appropriate contracts have been signed by you and filed with the necessary organizations.

EFFECTIVE COMMUNICATION DURING THE SESSION

Communication is the most important skill you have to develop to be successful. A useful starting point is to treat musicians with patience and respect. You will make your own life easier—and perhaps coax a special performance out of an artist.

Whether in your own studio or an outside studio, ensure that your artists are as comfortable as possible in their performing environments. Make sure there is enough light, the chairs are comfortable, coffee and other light beverages are available, the temperature in the studio is adequate, and the music is legible.

It is good practice and well worth the minimal financial investment to have light snacks or sandwiches around all of the time. If you are doing a jingle, station ID, or any other short session, coffee and light snacks are usually sufficient. On longer session(s), have more substantial food available. Make sure that you allow enough break time for everyone to feel rested and to have something to eat and drink. Your thoughtfulness will go a long way to building your reputation as a good employer.

SETUP AND REHEARSAL

Give the musicians and the engineer enough time to set up for recording. The drummer should come about an hour earlier in order to set up and get sounds. If the other artists are sitting around waiting for the drummer to finish setting up, they can lose their adrenaline and creative urge even before the session starts. Similarly, if you are recording rhythm tracks before any vocal tracks, you don't need to have the vocalists there until the rhythm tracks are finished. Plan the arrival and start time of each of the artists accordingly.

If the musicians are overdubbing to existing tracks, the engineer will supply a mix to the headphones. Ask the artists if they are comfortable with their headphone mixes and encourage their feedback, with the understanding that they may be sharing a mix with some of the other artists on the session and may have to compromise. It is not unusual for younger players to be afraid to speak up, simply because they are shy or do not know better. Sometimes this can result in a weaker performance than you might have expected.

When producing, I always ask for a set of headphones in the control room so that I can personally monitor the headphone mix. Occasionally, I will have the engineer put the headphone mix through the main control-room monitors so that we can hear what the performers are hearing. If you're getting less-than-perfect performances, the problem may be the headphone mix.

Once the headphone mix is set, rehearse the tracks and make sure that all of the pieces fit. Rehearsal techniques are a real art and are very important to recording success. The musicians must feel absolutely comfortable with every measure of the piece before they record. This will ensure a strong performance.

A common trick is to record the rehearsals without telling the performers that they are being recorded. It takes no time away from the session, and on rare occasions, you will get that magical performance that would have been lost otherwise. It is always a pleasure to tell musicians that you have the take that you need, even *before* they know they are recording.

DURING THE SESSION

Communicate with the performers throughout the session. Don't leave them waiting for feedback. If they finish playing and there is absolute silence from the control room, they may feel some anxiety. Make it a point to say *something* after each take, even if it is just that you're going to listen to what was just recorded.

If you are going to do another take, tell the performers why. Accentuate the positive points of what was just recorded, then mention the things that you would like performed differently on the next pass. Don't make a big deal of the problem, because no matter how small the error is, whoever made the mistake could very well be making a *huge* deal of it in their minds.

Likewise, don't have performers re-record tracks that they played perfectly on the last pass. If they did a great job, leave their track alone, and fix the tracks on which there were problems. For example, if the bassist "nails" the last take, but the guitarist played a few questionable chords, there is nothing gained by having the bassist play the track again. It might even be counterproductive, as you could lose the magic of the original bass track.

Being patient and learning how to communicate effectively will be one of your greatest attributes. The musicians/artists will respect you more if you guide their performances in the creation of a track that makes *them* proud. In my own career as a studio musician, I have on occasion silently questioned the decisions of the producer, only to hear the final mixes and realize that the producer was right. This is a producer that I am pleased to work for; he made me sound good!

You can also make things easier for your performers by being aware of what the instruments can do. That way, you won't waste session time learning what each instrument is capable of playing. Players will respect you enormously if your suggestions are musical and are play-able—but be sure that you know what to ask of your players.

As a final reminder: during the session, give performers adequate breaks. Breaks can be "official," or may take the form of the musi-cians coming into the control room to listen to the tracks on the monitors. This can be a refreshing diversion and will give performers a different perspective.

WHEN THINGS GO WRONG

Not surprisingly, there are times when, despite your best plans and intentions, things can get difficult. Remain calm and do what is necessary to keep the session moving. Occasionally, you will have to mediate quarrels between players. If this occurs, you must stop the behavior immediately and make it clear that the musician is there to record the music; any behavior that is less than professional will not be tolerated. Fortunately, if you do your research and hire the right performers, this will rarely happen, if at all. Professionals take great pride in their work and will always be punctual, barring any unfore-seen circumstances.

It is highly likely that at some point, you will encounter these unforeseen circumstances and have to think on your feet. For example, if a performer does not show up, accomplished producers pull out their contact lists and call the missing artist right away to find out what has happened. If the producer can't find the person, it's time for a contingency plan. There is no sense in worrying whether or not they are going to show up. Any responsible musician who *could* call the studio *would* call the studio.

There are many solutions to every problem. Think about the options and do what you feel is best. If a drummer doesn't show up, perhaps you have scratch drum tracks on the sequence and you can use those for the session. If you are working in a studio complex, there might be another drummer who can come in and do your session. You can try to find a player who lives nearby. Or just do the session with the click track and worry about the drums later. Whichever dilemma you face, you must look for the most efficient and productive solution.

From time to time, the performers may not give you an adequate track. What do you do when the singer is out of tune or the drummer is half a beat late? Trust your knowledge of the performers and your instincts in these cases. Ultimately, you have to determine if the problem is rectifiable or not, then act accordingly.

If a vocal track is not going well, start by trying to fix general problems. Vocalists need a comfortable setting, both sonically and environmentally. First, ask if they are comfortable. Is the temperature right? Is the lighting right? Would they like something to drink? Your sensitivity to their needs can go a long way toward creating a positive and productive environment.

You'll wonder how it is possible to have patience when the clock seems to be flying, the musicians are having difficulties, and the singer is out of tune. However, your impatience can very easily destroy the whole session. Even in the worst-case scenario, you have to pick up and reassemble the pieces as well as you can.

You do have to know when to call it quits—but without giving up too soon. Decisions made impatiently and impulsively aren't likely to be wise ones. When you have decided what you are going to do, make your decision the final decision. The only person that may have the right to change your mind is the client. I have occasionally seen clients willing to cover the extra expense for more studio time if they think there is a lot to be gained.

PRODUCING THE VOCAL TRACK

Once the performers are comfortable in their environment, pay close attention to the headphone mix. Singers must hear themselves at the proper level and in the proper ambience in order to create a meaningful performance. If, for example, the pitch is flat, one of the first things you can do, even without asking, is lower the vocals in the headphones. Often vocalists will hold back because they hear too much of themselves in the phones. Holding back results in a lack of breath support, which can lower the pitch. Conversely, if the pitch is sharp overall, I raise the headphone level slightly in order to compensate for the singers pushing too hard to hear themselves.

If the intonation is a little shaky, the best route is often to approach the track section by section, punching in to fix the problem areas. However, first determine how much time you have, because these "fix-it" solutions can be very time consuming and expensive.

I have found that the best approach for vocals is to record a complete version of the piece, ask the singer to come into the control room and listen with me, decide where the problem areas are, and fix those parts. If you have hired a professional and written your parts in the proper range, this should not take long.

If you still can't get a useable performance and you have spent what you feel is an adequate amount of time, you have to assess the time versus returns. If the track isn't improving, you may have to stop, then either hire another vocalist or digitally fix what you have.

SOLOISTS

Soloists, particularly vocalists, require specific attention, since they represent the primary musical focal point. If possible, do the solos at the end of the session as an overdub. In this way, the soloist can feel free to work without the pressure of the rest of the band waiting around.

Explain the concept for the solo even before the recording commences, and allow the soloist adequate time to give you what you need. If you have hired the right person, each performance will be good, and you can select the one that works best. It is not unusual for great studio players to rip out fantastic solos on every take, but a younger player might need some coaxing. Accentuate the positive and minimize the negative when discussing their performance. You can try to inspire the player by comparing what you want to a well-known player or by asking for a specific sound and concept. They might not show it, but they do want your help and guidance.

CALLING IT QUITS

One of the most difficult decisions that you may have to make is ending a session before a particular player has finished his or her track. There are many considerations that can lead to ending a session: a weak groove, players not playing what is written, tempos slowing down or speeding up, players having difficulty playing with the click track, or lack of musical teamwork by the performers.

To make your decision, you have to weigh many factors. Consider the ability of the performers; by continually doing many takes, will you get a better performance or would it be just luck? Consider the amount of time that is remaining, what is still to be recorded, and the importance of a particular track in the final product. Take into account the deadline, the budget for overtime (if any), and the ability to "fix it in the mix." The attitude and patience of the other performers on the session also will impact your decision, but perhaps even more importantly, consider the "vibe" or impressions of the client, if present.

All of these factors, many of which can be emotionally driven, have to be digested quickly and a decision made as to whether or not to continue. The more you work with performers, the quicker you will recognize what you can and cannot get from their performances. Learn to realize the point of "no gain" from both a musical and financial point of view.

If you are familiar with the players you have hired and know they are capable, but aren't delivering, try to get to the root of the problem. Make sure everything is comfortable technically and environmentally and that you have communicated your concepts effectively. Each case will be different and you will learn how to get the right performance. Be patient and concise, but don't push anything to the point of futility. If the players you have hired aren't experienced, aren't stylistically appropriate, or just aren't strong performers, there isn't much you can do other than accept what you have and apply what you've learned to your next session.

The ultimate success of your project boils down to your efforts. Be sure that you are completely prepared, little is left to chance, and you are knowledgeable about all areas of the production and your own compositions. Confidence in your work and the people you hire should give you peace of mind that you can handle just about anything that happens during the production—and still create a wonderful-sounding recording.

PROJECT 6.1. BUILD YOUR ROSTER OF MUSICIANS

List all the musicians you know who would be good choices for a professional project. Do you have at least three players on all rhythm section instruments? Do you have at least three male and three female vocalists? Do you have at least three players who can double on various woodwinds: different saxes, flute, clarinet? Do you have coverage on other commonly required instruments, such as trumpet and violin? Evaluate your list, and come up with a plan for finding contacts where you have gaps. You want musicians on your roster before you have an immediate need.

CONCLUSION

Live musicians can make a tremendous impact on your recording projects. It is critical that you have a strong roster of excellent musicians to call upon, with good coverage of all major instruments. It is also important that you treat them well enough at the sessions so that they will be eager to work with you again.

CHAPTER **7**

Anatomy of a Writing Gig

NOW, LET'S PUT IT ALL TOGETHER. In this chapter, we will review all phases of finding and fulfilling gigs and getting paid for them. Details vary, but the general process goes something like this.

1. GROUNDWORK

Before you get your next writing job, a lot has already taken place. You've set up shop, developed your reputation, and made a lot of contacts. Your demo kit has made the rounds. Musicians know you, as do art directors within corporations or agencies. Maybe you've got a degree in music. Your studio functions fine; all bugs have been worked out. You've produced your own library of musical ideas, with drumbeats, melodies, sounds, and other reusable audio tracks, to make the creation process easier. From a technology and knowledge standpoint, you're ready to go.

Your name is out there. You are easily findable, with a Web site and listing in local telephone directories. Your business has a name, a history of completed projects, and all the marketing items discussed in the previous chapter. In other words, when a client finds that they have a need, you already have an existing presence in the marketplace.

Ideally, this includes your name being in the client's address book, preferably with a sample of your work in their files. If you are known to him, a potential client might not place a "call for demos" at all. He might call you, and only you, and say, "Mike, we need some music. Here's the video. Send me thirty seconds of hip-hop to underscore it." This is the most efficient usage of everyone's time, and your marketing goal is to establish as many of these relationships as you can, so that you don't have to compete for projects.

A product will be released, a radio-show format will be changed to require stingers or bumpers, a videogame will be produced, or a TV show pilot will be screened. Music is needed, and someone has the potential to request it from you. Connecting with these people is critical, and it should happen well in advance of specific projects. There are essentially four types of contacts who will be instrumental in getting you gigs: corporate employees, account managers at ad agencies, music supervisors at jingle houses, and agents.

Larger corporations may employ an in-house music supervisor to coordinate the music, particularly for commercials, presentations, Web sites, and so on. There may be an in-house Marketing/ Promotion department, the director of which may be responsible for finding writers.

Many companies still work with outside advertising agencies. At these firms, the person hiring composers might be called an account executive or project manager. In the film/TV industries, the coordinator might be called a music supervisor, though there's the same trend towards multitasking there as in music, so the director and music supervisor might be the same person. Any of these coordinators might call individual writers, or they might call "jingle houses."

Large jingle houses, with several employed writers, are not as common as they once were. Some still exist, but today's equivalents generally subcontract out to independent production houses, such as you. The coordinator might be called an account executive, project manager, or music supervisor.

Some companies contact agents, rather than individual writers. Agents connect writers with clients. They take a percentage of the profits, often around 15 percent. An agency might handle various types of talent, including performing musicians, voiceover specialists, actors, composers, and so on. Some agents are independent, and some work in groups.

2. CALL FOR DEMOS

When the project hits, there will be a call for demos. In some cases, where there's an established work history, an account manager might just call a known writer and ask if they can take the project.

In other cases, there is a competitive process, where the account manager contacts several writers or publicly advertises for interested writers to submit demos. They will specify the parameters of the job and its compensation. Turnaround time is often very tight—often a day or two.

In answering a call for a demo, writers scramble to put something together quickly, of high quality. A TV commercial or videogame call might include a QuickTime file of the video, to which the writers will synchronize their music. Or, there may be a general description, such as "fifteen seconds of a hip-hop groove to underscore a voiceover, with a sax fill in the last four seconds."

The client chooses the best demo and forwards its writer a contract. In some cases, there is a small compensation for writers who submitted a demo that didn't get chosen.

3. NEGOTIATING A CONTRACT

Contracts specify project parameters and compensation. It is becoming more prevalent that commercial music work is based on the buyout model. There is a one-time fee for the entire project. For these, there are no royalties. It is still common—particularly in larger unionized projects—that residuals/royalties will be paid beyond the initial performance cycle.

If you have an existing working relationship with the client, they may send you the contract when they request the demo, just to keep things simple.

4. DELIVERY/REVISION

You'll likely get feedback to the demo. In many kinds of commercial music work, production costs are included in the writer's payment, so you will be delivering a final, mixed version(s) of the music, generally on CD. A client may request changes in instrumentation, volume, business, or any other parameters. These days, selected demos are generally so close to being finals that requested revisions are likely to be minor, but they could happen.

Larger projects, such as films and videogames, might have a spotting session, at this stage, to discuss the exact musical requirements. There might be a temp score of music in the general style that the client wants you to imitate, for the final version.

Another common step in going from demo to final is to replace MIDI lead lines with live ones. If there are scratch vocals on the demo, they will be replaced by the final vocals. A more detailed mix will be done, for the final.

The contract is critical here because it specifies the resources you will need to complete the job. Your production costs will be included in your fee. If after you deliver a proposed "final," the client says "Let's have two sax melodies, not just one," you can point to the contract and insist upon additional compensation, if the contract specified just one lead sax line.

5. COLLECTING PAYMENT

You'll likely get paid a percentage of the fee when the contract gets signed and the balance upon delivery of the final. It's standard to get paid within thirty days of final delivery.

Fees are generally all inclusive from the writing through the final master. It includes paying any live musicians, studio time, and mixing.

CASE STUDY: DOG FOOD COMMERCIAL

Let's look at an example of how this might go.

Say a company creates a new kind of dog food and is developing a television commercial as part of its advertising campaign. Here's a typical scenario showing how the music will get made.

Tuesday: Call for Demo

The product director in charge of dog food calls their ad agency and requests an ad. The agency's art director (AD) first oversees the production of the script and video. Two tasks remain: the music and the voiceover.

The AD thinks that a jazz score would be best, and so goes through her file of demos from various writers and chooses three with jazz credentials. You are one of them. She e-mails you a link to a QuickTime version of the video and asks you to send a demo of some music for it. It's thirty seconds long.

You call her, and have an initial discussion regarding creative direction, the music's purpose and function, the project budget, and the timetable.

It's a good gig: you'll get $500 for submitting the demo or $7,500 plus residuals for the completed recording, if they choose you; the 50 percent residual of $3,750 will be paid for every subsequent 13-week cycle. The demo is due by the end of the week, and the final will be due by the following Wednesday. Sometimes, time frames are much tighter.

Immediately, you go to work producing the demo. You actually have a half-completed track from a different project that never got used, and you decide to recycle that. It's just a rhythm section part, so you add a MIDI sax part playing the melody, which you expect to be replaced by a live player, if you get the gig.

You produce a highly professional-sounding recording. It is carefully mixed, polished, and suits the video perfectly. It takes you about eight hours, from writing to mixing.

Thursday: Demo Delivery

You print a CD label on your laser printer, put it in a jewel case, and courier it to the Art Director with a polite cover letter thanking her for thinking of you and your hope that the music meets her needs, and expressing a willingness to change any aspect of it if she requires it.

Friday: Selection

The Dog Food Director chooses your demo, and so the AD sends $500 to one of the other two writers; the third writer opted out. The one who submitted the losing demo immediately uses his attempt in another project that pays $10,000, and so he's relieved to have been rejected.

The AD sends you the contract. The terms are $7,500 for 30 seconds of music, in a lump sum, plus 50 percent residuals. You'll get half the money now and half upon acceptance of the final.

In some cases, the process might actually begin with the contract. If the AD had a tighter turnaround, and if she and the Dog Food Director had worked with you before and knew that you'd be a suitable writer for this project, they might not bother with the call for demos from multiple writers. The AD might just hire you—call you and say, "Mike, can you do a thirty-second dog food commercial? Jazz score, $7,500, I'll e-mail you the link and fax over the usual contract."

You sign the contract and fax it back to her.

Monday: Creation of Final

The AD says your demo was great, but the sax solo was too busy in certain parts for the voiceover. Also, could you use an electric bass, not an acoustic bass sound? And the client wants the sax to answer with a funny noise, after the dog barks.

You say "Sure." You hire a great tenor saxophone player to rerecord the melody. He nails it in two takes, which takes about twenty minutes of his time, in the studio. You give him $300 in cash on his way out. He smiles and tells you to call him again anytime.

You fix a couple lingering details, and do a somewhat more meticulous mix.

Tuesday: Revision

You cut a new CD, label it nicely, and FedEx it to the AD, along with your invoice.

Wednesday: Project Completion

The AD loves it and sends it to the Dog Food Director. He loves it too, so he approves the final, and the ad agency's in-house post-production engineer adds the voiceover. In twenty-nine days, their accounting office mails you the remainder of your fee.

Thirteen Weeks Later

The ad is successful, so it runs again. You get a residual check for $3,750.

This is the basic process. At all stages, the writer must try to understand what the client needs and to deliver that. Writing commercial music is different than writing for purely artistic purposes because the product must conform to the client's needs and expectations. Writing for a client is a unique way of thinking about music, and it requires special sensitivity and attention. And you must be able to capture, in your music, what is emotionally exciting about dog food.

PROJECT 7.1. GETTING CONNECTED

Who knows that you are available to write music for their projects? How will you add to their roster of who to call? Come up with a plan to become known to at least ten people capable of hiring you.

WRITING FOR THE CLIENT

As you might see from reviewing the above process, the contemporary writer must also act as his own producer. During the creative process, he must imagine himself as the client's advocate, and produce a product to the client's specifications—regardless of the writer's personal musical tastes. Let's look at how this process of production works.

Production starts from the moment that conceptualization and composition begin. Regardless of how we write, whether it is with the piano, guitar, synths, or voice, we are *producing* our music as we compose. We imagine what we would *like* to hear, and often hear the final orchestrations and mixes as we write. The shaping of the music, the building of tension and release, the use of musical texture and color, the concept of ambience and mood, and the preliminary concepts for the recording and mixing evolve during the writing stages—and all of this, for the commercial writer, is aimed toward pleasing the client.

Before music could be reproduced electronically, composers "produced" their music primarily through the use of orchestration and venue. The orchestration created the textures, timbres, and musical emotion, while the venue created the ambience. For example, Gustav Mahler was a master "producer." The passion of the music he conceived was clearly defined, not only in the notes, but also in the orchestration and in how he envisioned the ambience of the concert hall. For example, if he wanted the trumpets to sound as if they were "calling" in the distance, they would play offstage. Today, we could use reverb to create the same effect.

Although technology is different and orchestration styles and the melding of different ethnic influences have changed the sounds of music, the fundamental role of composer/producers hasn't changed too much over time. Like all of our musical ancestors, the writer/ producer's goal is to bring the music to the people in the best way possible, while also making enough to pay the rent—and that means pleasing the clients. Here's a three-step process to help achieve your compositional goals as a commercial writer/producer.

STEP 1. DEFINE THE CLIENT'S GOAL FOR THE PROJECT

In commercial music, this is rule number 1: *A successful composition meets the client's needs.* At the outset of every project, have a discussion with your clients to clarify their goals for the project. Ask them a few questions: What image do they want the music to convey? What effect do they want the music to have on listeners? Who are the customers for their products? And, importantly: what is the budget and the timetable for completion? Take clear notes. Also, get some samples of music they have used in the past. Knowing the previous work of your clients and learning about the work of writers and production houses they have used in the past will help you understand what they are looking for from you.

Be sure you understand the client's concept of how your music will enhance his or her work. If you are writing to picture, spend as much time as necessary with the director and music supervisor to determine their goals for the music. Is the music intended to be in the foreground or background? For example, if the music will be particularly prominent in a dialog-free scene in a television show or film, your composition will need to have more presence. In a scene like this, the music can aid the visual in a very powerful way, creating emotion and ambience in conjunction with the picture.

If you are not clear on what would work in a particular scene, try to find out what the client thinks might work. Give "musical bait" for the client to expand on. For example, "What do you think about a symphonic orchestra type of sound for this scene?" By using a concrete example, you can prompt discussion that may provide the guidance you need. Let the client suggest the initial musical direction and concept, then assure him or her that you can turn their concepts into reality.

If you are unfamiliar with the musical genre the client envisions, do your research. Encourage them to be specific. If your client requests something "smart and sizzling" for the trailer of their new television show, ask for a musical example of what they mean by that. With this knowledge in hand, the writing and production should be much easier, because you can find ways to emulate the effects that the client likes in the "example" music.

Be sure to ask the client about the target audience. Demographics are a powerful indicator of what the music should be. In commercial advertising, the ad agencies know their target audience and plan the whole campaign around it, placing ads in carefully selected magazines and on television and radio at particular time periods during certain types of shows. Knowing these "targets" will help you formulate the concepts for your music. For a lesson in demographics, compare the music written for MTV advertising to the music written for advertising on the Food Network.

Many times, the purpose of the composition will dictate how much time you have to spend on the writing and production. Is it for a film score or a short radio jingle? If you are writing for the tight-deadline world of film, television, or advertising, you may find that you have to sacrifice some musical creativity to musical purpose. Your goal may be to create an effective product that is supportive in nature, rather than to produce compositional originality. Go with your musical instincts in these cases. The study of commercial music and its related compositional clichés will afford you a quick start in these fields. Most successful writers in these fields can churn out the music very quickly because they know the genres.

Occasionally in the commercial music field, your client will request that the music have some kind of relationship to a particular band or style. If the client wants a track in a disco groove à la Donna Summer, the development of your song is underway before you write. If the client wants a groove of a particular Prince song, buy the album that contains that track and learn it.

Sometimes, the client may want you to be almost exact in the duplication of a particular song or style in order to avoid paying synchronization licensing fees. However, *you* have to know the limits, since you will likely be legally responsible. Learn what you can and cannot use. Using someone else's melody violates copyright law. You can transcribe exact drum grooves and timbral content from an original and then change the harmony and melody to ensure that you are not breaking any laws. Some similarities between two songs can be obvious, yet still not infringe copyright. For example, just by duplicating a well-known style of vocal harmony, you imply a relationship to an artist and musical period in which they performed. That does not infringe on a copyright. However, "image" can be protected. Sounding like Bobby Darin on "Mack the Knife," even unintentionally, can be a potential infringement. Copyright law clearly defines the boundaries of copyright infringement. (The U. S. Copyright Office Web site is http://lcweb. loc.gov/copyright.)

STEP 2. PLAN YOUR COMPOSITION

Once you understand what the client wants, it's your job to figure out how to provide it. To help clarify your compositional approach, ask yourself these fundamental questions:

- How do the compositional areas of key, form and structure, rhythmic style (groove), orchestration, and improvisation help to shape the mood or ambience?
- When appropriate, how does lyrical content establish the meaning of the song and how does the music support this powerful element?
- How will the recording process enhance the song?
- How will technology in the recording and mix process cement the final image that the composition is trying to express?
- Which musicians will be best to perform this particular piece?
- How can I get the best product for my budget?
- If writing to picture, how will the composition fit the visual and help convey its meaning?
- If writing jingles, how will the music fit the product image and target the proper audience?

Most importantly, know what effect you want to achieve. This will determine the instruments you use and the harmonic and melodic structures you select to conjure a particular image. For example, if the client is looking for a Gothic sound, you might produce the part so it sounds like a church organ with big reverb.

Of course, you must consider the budget. If you were writing for a large orchestra doing a "sweetening" session—a session in which strings, horns, or other additional instruments are overdubbed onto existing tracks—your compositional approach would be much different than working with a loop and other samples. Your budget and your client's requirements are the critical factors in determining how the track will ultimately be produced.

As you compose, think about the **soundscape** you wish to create. In painting, the term "landscape" represents an entire visual image and its emotional impact. In composition, "soundscape" is a term used to describe the entire aural image. Remember, you can't rely solely on recording technology to accomplish this, so you have to write with the soundscape in mind.

Before you start, have an idea of the orchestration and textural devices that you will use. It can also be helpful to sketch out a chord progression or melodic motif that can be used as the basis of the composition. Compositional factors such as harmonic progression, groove (rhythmic feel), melody, harmonic rhythm, tempo, style, textures, and key of the piece will determine much of the soundscape.

Let's say, for example, that you are writing a cue for a movie scene set in 1850, involving a quiet, revealing moment between a man and a woman sitting in a parlor. The mood and visual is very aristocratic. Place yourself in that period. Ask yourself what music would most effectively support the visual, the mood of the discussion, the overall positive or negative elements of the scene, and the personalities of the characters involved.

A solo oboe, which evokes a very serious, contemplative, and sometimes lonely feeling, accompanied by lush strings underneath, all set in a minor key, might be appropriate. The ambience would be intimate but not *too* close—a longer reverb for the oboe, and the strings fully orchestrated in the middle registers. If recording live strings, use close miking to evoke an intimate sound. This combines the *oneness* of the individuals and the intimacy of the environment and the moment.

STEP 3. ORCHESTRATION: LIVE INSTRUMENTS VS. MIDI

Decide whether you will use live instruments or MIDI, or a combination of both. The decision is based primarily on the budget, but client's demands, musical context, orchestrational ideas, deadlines, recording convenience, your MIDI skills, and the versatility of your project studio will also dictate your decision. If your budget is very small, you are apt to do a MIDI/sample recording without needing to hire live musicians.

Knowing that you will be recording live musicians will steer your writing and production in several respects. From a production standpoint, the sound of live musicians will often be different than the sound of sequencers. The recording and mixing of live musicians is generally more challenging than that of sequenced tracks. Remember that a sequence that sounds good might sound horrible when played by live musicians.

However, hiring great players will always assure you great performances and creative additions to your music that you might not have otherwise considered or expected. You can leave a lot of the musical creation to the players by just giving them general parts on which they can expand.

If you are writing vocals, knowing the singer(s) is of prime importance. Male or female, the character of their voices, their vocal ranges and control, the styles in which they sing convincingly, their ability to blend with others in background parts, how well they deliver lyrical content, their sight-reading abilities, and how well they take direction, represent important considerations.

MIDI-only recording presents challenges of its own. If you are not a keyboard player, it can be difficult to get a live feel from your music. Your recording will most likely be in **step time**, or note-by-note input into the sequencer. This can sound very mechanical. For authentic feels, your best bet in recording MIDI-only is to play the parts in **real time** and then edit afterwards to correct any mistakes. Your composition and subsequent production is the determining factor for how to record MIDI-only. Your best option may be to hire a keyboardist.

If financially feasible, the combination of live and MIDI instruments is an efficient method of producing. Regardless of the instrument(s) you play, you can generally add life to a MIDI track with a live performance. If you are a guitar player, don't hesitate to play guitar over your MIDI tracks to give them a live feel. You can even use a MIDI guitar to input parts and give them a live-performance feel.

For more information, see chapter 10, "Composing with MIDI."

HONING YOUR COMPOSITIONAL SKILLS

As a commercial composer, you must always expand your knowledge of music. Learn, listen, write, and practice. Listen to music with "big ears" for compositional and production elements. It's like viewing a painting from a distance to admire it in its entirety. Only until you step up very close can you see the enormous detail and meticulous craftsmanship that went into the work. Every brushstroke has a purpose on the painting and every note played by every instrument also is a small part of the greater whole. But the listener, even if he or she doesn't look under the microscope, will hear your music as the sum of all of these countless details. It is this detail for which you are responsible.

Be a student and study writing. Listen to music critically to uncover how composers have derived emotion, and use some of the same elements in your music. You might be called upon to write music for anything at any time. The best orchestration lessons are often the ones you get by listening to music from *all* eras. Study the scores for some of the best-known classical pieces and follow along with the music. From these studies, you will acquire a complete palette of orchestrational colors. Each era can be defined by a particular sound.

The changing technology and invention of new instruments, recording, mass media, and the Internet all seem to compact the creation of music into parcels of sound and quality. For example, the 1960s have a sound and style distinct from any other decade. It is not enough to use synthesizer sounds to duplicate these elements and merely guess at how you *think* the style would have sounded. Your music will sound authentic only if researched and reproduced authentically, adhering to the musical and production elements from the period as closely as possible.

As a composer, you should have a general understanding of all the instruments that are available and know how to write for them. Be aware of the ranges of instruments, the different sounds they can create, how instruments sound alone or in combination, the mood that each timbre creates, and the appropriate types of music for each instrument.

Use other recordings and compare your work against the highest quality and most successful work in the marketplace. When you listen, use headphones to recognize the details of the recording techniques. Television, film music, and jingles all have unique mixing techniques and emphases. By listening carefully and analytically, you will soon establish a set of criteria by which to judge your work. Further, you will develop new skills that you can add to your existing production "toolbox."

VERSATILITY

Another thing I write on the whiteboard is:

The days of being a one-trick pony are long gone. Contemporary writers need to be open-minded, accepting, and willing to learn a variety of styles of music—to be jacks-of-all-trades, and masters of a few. We need to be convincing in all styles. A writer can't say "Hip-hop is just a fad, I thought it would fade in the 1970s." We need to be able to write a hip-hop track, and a country track, and a classical track.

A common way that would-be writers are self-defeating is in being snobbish and closed minded. But you don't need to like a musical style to produce it effectively. There is something to appreciate about every style.

For example, some elitist musicians may want to hate pop music. I try to convince them to listen to it for what it is, and to see how it fulfills its purpose. The productions are generally incredible. The way these recordings are constructed is genius. It's not an accident of people haphazardly putting pieces together; it's painstakingly crafted, and it appeals wildly to a major demographic.

Professional writers must be able to understand and recreate it. If a client calls for a Britney Spears–style track, and says there's ten grand in it, you're not going to say, "No, that music sucks, I just write jazz fusion." We need to be able to do it, and to do it sincerely—to appreciate how great everything is, even "Achy Breaky Heart."

If you can see what's good in all music, you'll be able to make a good impression on a wide variety of clients. If you can talk knowledgeably with a potential client, when they want a piece written in a country music, or hip-hop, or pop music style, you can then build a rapport, and that will get you the gig.

Coming up to speed on a variety of styles is a critical aspect of your research. The more you can do, the more gigs you will get.

PROJECT 7.2. DEVELOPING VERSATILITY

List styles of music that you don't know much about, or that you actively dislike. Then produce two short pieces in that style: one lasting for thirty seconds, the other for three minutes. Research the style, and make your music sound authentic. Do this at least once every few months.

CONCLUSION

When a need for music comes into the marketplace, you need to be poised to fulfill it. You need to be known to the people who hire music writers, you need to have the necessary skills and connections, and you need the mechanisms for producing the actual recordings. By developing each of these capabilities, when opportunity strikes, you will be ready.

PART II

Technology

The second part of this book discusses recording technology and strategies in detail. It will give you an overview of the process and then much detail regarding its stages—from a writer's perspective. Mastery requires time, so be patient as you grow.

CHAPTER **8**

Recording Studios

THE CRAFT OF PRODUCING A RECORDING IS AS COMPLEX as the craft of writing music. There are infinite ways to manipulate sound and an endless amount of hardware you might buy. In this chapter, I'll map out an overview of the processes, and expand on it in later chapters. Check the Resources appendix for more detailed information about all aspects of engineering.

Twenty years ago, writers recorded their music in outside recording studios. First, they'd compose the music and copy parts for musicians. Everyone would meet at a recording studio, and there would be a process of recording, overdubbing, and then mixing the tracks. Dedicated engineers recorded and mixed the performances, and separate producers supervised the sessions.

With the rise of the personal computer, MIDI, and affordable software, the processes changed. Often, we writers now engineer and produce our own music. The separate step of notating individual parts is less common, and writers instead perform many of the parts themselves, into their computers, using MIDI controllers, drum machines, synthesizers, sound libraries, and other sound sources. Live performers are used for lead parts and vocals, but other tracks are often created electronically. Rudimentary mixing occurs early. Best practice is to use templates, where basic levels are set before you actually start writing.

Of course, different writers will have their own approaches. Some writers still think in terms of notation and *step recording*, where they program the MIDI note by note. Other writers find it more natural to begin the process with existing loops.

But we all need to be our own engineers, and we all need to have our own home studios—even if the project eventually goes to a professional studio for fine-tuning later on. Writers require engineering skills to produce commercial music.

About ten years ago, affordable home studios began to rival the big studios, particularly for commercial work such as jingles. Beginning writers might find that they do all their work in their home studios. More experienced writers may find themselves sometimes working in bigger studios, as well. Each has its advantages, and we'll discuss them in more detail throughout the following chapters.

Home Studio	Professional Studio
Low cost	More room
More convenience	Better-sounding equipment (generally)
Less time pressure	Improved sound isolation
Less setup time	Large instruments, such as grand piano, harpsichord, Hammond B3
	Staff engineer
	Microphone collection
	Variety of outboard gear

Professional studios still have their place. They can afford to invest in better gear and facilities than most individuals can, and it's usually possible to get better-sounding recordings out of them than you could at a typical home studio. But home studios can produce recordings that are good enough for most purposes. Software programs use the traditional look and feel of their hardware predecessors, so learning the ins and outs of a major audio editing program will simultaneously teach you how to use the gear at a professional studio.

In the end, cost and convenience usually win, over minor differences in sound quality, particularly when the goal is to sell dog food, rather than create an artistic masterwork. So develop your engineering chops, and build your studio. The remainder of this book will help to get you started.

THE RECORDING PROCESS

The recording process includes everything involved in realizing a musical composition into electronic form. Sounds get organized in an electronic medium. The client then takes that electronic file and broadcasts it, often pairing it with video or other forms of media.

Years ago, the sounds on a recording were exclusively recorded, using microphones or plugging electronic instruments directly into a recording device. This is also called *tracking*.

Contemporary writing techniques combine newly recorded sounds with existing sounds, often controlled by MIDI devices. These sounds are manipulated and combined together in a process known as *mixing*.

Sounds from tracking sessions, recorded music libraries, and synthesizers all get combined in a recording studio. A recording studio is essentially a very complex tape recorder.

There are three types of components:

1. **Audio capturers.** Acoustic sounds are captured by microphones, while sounds from electric instruments (electric guitars, sound modules, synthesizers, etc.) are often plugged into hardware (audio cards, patch bays, etc.) that routes the sound to a sound manipulation device, where the sounds are organized in tracks. A track is an independently editable recording stream. If you had a separate track for a singer and a guitar part, you could edit the recordings of each separately, perhaps making the vocals louder in relation to the guitar part, or deciding to mute the guitar part for a section while the vocals sound unchanged.

2. **Audio manipulators.** The essential sound manipulator is often called a *mixing board*, and they come in hardware and software forms, of various sizes and degrees of power. In a professional studio, it is likely a *recording console*—a large desk with hundreds of controls. In a home studio, it's likely a software program, such as Pro Tools, Digital Performer, Logic, Sonar, Reason, and so on. These programs or devices coordinate volume balancing, stereo panning, and sound coloring of each recording channel.

3. **Audio storers.** These are often called *multitrack devices* because they can keep several recorded tracks isolated and individually editable. Nowadays, most engineers use computer hard disks as their multitrack devices, particularly in home studios. Multitrack tape is still in use, but it is becoming rarer.

The modern process of creating a recording generally happens in two phases:

1. **Audio gathering.** Parts get recorded, programmed in MIDI, or assembled from sound libraries. The order is generally drums, bass, comping instruments (guitar, keyboard, organ), lead instruments, background vocals, lead vocals, special effects. This will likely include an *overdub session*, which is where selections of parts can be rerecorded after the fact, to correct errors or to capture new possibilities. We'll discuss microphone technique in chapter 9.

2. **Mixing and mastering.** *Mixing* includes all aspects of editing and manipulating sounds, from balancing relative volumes for each instruments to fine-tuning instrument tones. In mixing, an engineer can have a profound effect on how the gathered sounds are expressed.

   After the music is mixed and sounds great, a stereo final mix is produced. (Film also mixes in several different formats, including 5.1, 7.1, and 7.2). This can then be recorded onto a CD, compressed into an MP3 and e-mailed, or delivered in various other ways.

   Mastering is the process of finalizing the product for its particular format. Mastering can be an extremely complex, painstaking process, or it can be a quick last step. In the record industry, *mastering* is the process of fine-tuning completed mixes to sound consistent on a recording, and it is often completed by a different engineer.

All these tasks are done in a recording studio.

STUDIO SPACES

The term "studio" may be a fancy name for the room in your basement where you compose music and experiment with effects software until the wee hours. But to the outside world, it's a business. So, you need to make it look like one. Once the business starts rolling in, you'll no doubt have clients come to your studio, so you want to ensure that it looks the part.

As a beginning writer/producer, your goal should be to build a studio that is within your budget, but that allows you to write, produce, and engineer professional-quality recordings. The studio frequently includes the physical space in which you record the music, as well as the office space in which you conduct the business.

If your studio is in your home, it is wise to keep the office and studio area as separate from the living part of your house as possible. It can be challenging to produce music in a home studio while family life is going on around you. The creative and business space should be a place for uninterrupted creative and business work.

I am a believer in setting up an attractive space, decorated well with an intimate yet businesslike appearance that will suit visiting artists and clients alike. These are the ideal places to meet with your clients and make a great impression. As a studio owner, I enjoyed having potential clients come to my studio for the first time. It was optimized for their comfort, and offered easy access to my demo reel, a set of my favorite CDs and other reference recordings, and letters of recommendation and thanks.

Amenities such as a working kitchen, fresh coffee, a clean washroom, comfortable seating, accessible parking, the ease of loading in musical equipment, communication access (such as fax machines, Internet, and telephones), a comfortable lounge area, and proximity to public transportation, all make it easier to manage your business and record music. The drummer who has to leave a car double-parked on a busy thoroughfare while hauling a drum kit up nine flights of stairs will not be as content as the drummer who pulls up to a door adjacent to the studio and can park just a few feet away. If you are looking for a new studio space, these are important elements to look for.

PROFESSIONAL STUDIOS

A professional recording studio will have five basic elements: the recording area, the multitrack machines/computer, the control room, the console, and outboard gear. (Studios come in many sizes and shapes, but for the purposes of this discussion, I am using a layout typical of a large studio. This helps to visualize the "virtual studio" and the necessary signal routing.)

The studio area. The recording area, where performers play, is often referred to as the "studio." This area might also include an *isolation booth*, a small soundproof room used to completely separate a sound source during recording, so that microphones only pick up sounds from a single instrument.

All studios need certain equipment:

- a microphone collection with microphone stands
- direct boxes and cables
- headphones so that the artists can hear each other and previously recorded material

A studio with more space and resources may also include large instruments and equipment, such as a grand piano, bass and guitar amps, or a Hammond organ and Leslie speaker. It is common to find movable sound barriers (referred to as gobos or baffles) to create isolation and minimize sound transfer within the studio.

Control room. The control room is made up of three distinct peripherals: the multitrack equipment, the console, and outboard gear. It is here that the engineer works. Most often, the producer will also work in the control room.

Multitrack equipment. This is the device onto which all of the audio tracks are first recorded. The multitrack system is most likely your computer and music production software, but it can be a tape machine, as well.

The console. The console is the hub of the recording studio. It routes audio signal to each area of the recording environment. In a large studio, the console is most likely an analog/digital piece of hardware through which all parts of the studio interconnect. The virtual consoles contained in software packages are no different in their fundamental function. One advantage of the analog console, as shown in the following diagram, is its access to all areas of the mix simultaneously. For example, when mixing, it is possible to make adjustments to many faders at once. In the virtual world you can only adjust one element at a time, typically with your mouse or interface. However, many companies are now manufacturing control surfaces for software-based recording. These pieces of hardware are connected directly to the computer, and are designed to duplicate the functions and appearance of a traditional console.

Traditional studio floor plan. In many modern studios, the computer covers the functions of the console, outboard-gear rack, 2-track machines, and the multitrack recorder.

This floor plan shows a typical large multitrack recording facility designed to record live instruments. While most modern studios are computer based, understanding the traditional studio configuration helps you understand the underlying order of the "virtual" studio.

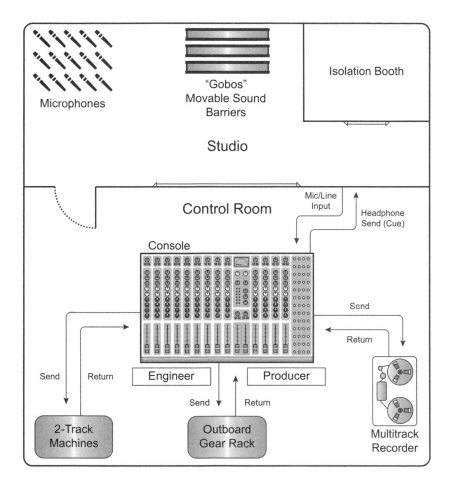

HOME STUDIOS

Home studios are like professional studios in many ways, though the spaces are often simpler, particularly when you are starting out and don't have the funds for massive carpentry and reworking. Creating your studio might be the most significant expense of your career, and it's important to invest appropriately in it.

Before you start assembling or expanding your studio, create a budget. Simplest, for a beginning writer still paying off student loans, is to start with something like this, and then add to it. Here's a fairly bare-bones studio for $8,300. You could shave a few dollars off of it by buying used gear, but not a lot.

Computer	$ 2000
Monitor	$ 700
Recording Software	$ 500
Speakers	$ 500
Headphone	$ 100
Audio Interface	$ 500
MIDI Interface	$ 300
Controller Keyboard	$2,000
Synth Module/Software Synthesizer	$ 500
Cables	$ 200
Table/Chair for equipment	$ 700
Miscellaneous (headphones, direct boxes, headphone splitter boxes, etc.)	$ 300
Total	**$8,300**

Here's a similar setup for $27,000. Notice how it's not much different, but already, the cost increases fairly dramatically. That's the nature of studios. Expenses creep in, so keep your overall budget handy whenever you consider adding new gear.

NEW EQUIPMENT EXPENSES

Faster Computer	$3,500
Monitor	$ 700
Software for sequencing, editing, notation, recording	$2,000
Speakers	$ 500
Digital Interface	$2,000
Digital Recording Console	$7,800
Midi Interface	$ 300
Better Controller Keyboard	$2,800
Sampler Module	$1,000
Synth Module	$1,900
Condenser Microphone	$ 500
More Cables	$ 300
Hardware Compressor	$1,000
Hardware Microphone Preamp	$1,000
Table/Chair for equipment	$ 700
Soundproofing for recording room	$ 500
More miscellaneous (headphones, direct boxes, headphone splitter boxes, etc.)	$ 500
Total Budget	**$27,000**

Know the source and amount of your capital. It is so important to set limitations for the studio. If you aren't going to be recording a lot of live instruments, you don't have to buy a lot of microphones. If you are going to be using your computer as your mix platform, it won't be necessary to spend a lot on a console. You can find a lot of used furniture and office equipment. You also must budget for office supplies, furnishings, communications systems, studio-equipment maintenance, research materials, and CDs. If your home needs to be modified to create a studio space, that's obviously going to be a major additional expense.

SOUND ISOLATION

Sound isolation is particularly important in a home studio. If you don't live alone, it is very likely that that there will be many times that you will be working while others are trying to sleep. Unless your studio is in a separate building, there really is no way to completely eliminate noise. However, there are several things that you can do to minimize noise.

If you are constructing a studio from an empty space, use as much sound insulation as possible inside of the walls. Close any vents. If your room is already built, then use as much sound-absorbent material on the walls and ceiling as possible.

If you have the space, consider setting up an isolation booth. It is quite often used for vocals when recorded live with a band. The "iso" booth is also used frequently for drums, which tend to bleed into other microphones. This gives the engineer and producer more flexibility at mix time to control the overall sound and ambience. (This will be discussed later on.) If you don't have room for an isolation booth, you can use movable sound barriers ("gobos") to create isolation. You can purchase gobos from any pro audio store that supplies high-end studio equipment, or you can make them yourself. Try using rolls of foam rubber covered with decorative fabric. Also, you can buy cheap lumber, construct frames to enclose the foam rubber, then cover the frames with fabric. Your budget will dictate what materials you can use. It isn't a good idea to buy the dedicated acoustic foam insulation squares. At approximately $100 each, they may be beyond the reach of anyone starting out. Be creative!

INDUSTRY SPOTLIGHT:
CHOOSING AN OUTSIDE STUDIO

There will be times when your home studio will not be equipped to handle a project's requirements. For those occasions, you'll need to know about the studios in your area. Visit these facilities, ask to hear demos, get rate sheets, and develop working relationships with the owner/operators. Here are some tips on deciding which studio to use.

What do you need? You need the best you can afford. If you are willing to work in off-peak hours or book blocks of time, you usually will save money. If you are recording music to visuals, you will definitely need a studio equipped to play and watch the video in synch with the music. Do you need a grand piano or an orchestra-sized room? Do you need a studio with several isolation booths for vocals, drums, and narration? Plan ahead and be sure the studio can meet your needs.

Also check into how well the studio can accommodate your digital files. Life is easier when you can bring digital transfer devices, such as CD-Rs, DVD-Rs, portable hard drives, and so on, that contain all of your sampled tracks, your MIDI tracks converted to digital audio, and the live tracks that you have already recorded. You just pop it into the studio's computer, and you are up and running.

How much can you afford? If you have only $500 budgeted for total studio time, and the studio wants $700, tell them what you can afford and stay within your guidelines. Quite often they will be accommodating, but ask about hidden costs like setup fees, rental for outboard gear, musical instruments, synchronization equipment, and special microphones.

Studio specialties. Some studios focus primarily on album work, others on film and television, and still others on jingle work. Book the right one for the right job.

Studio amenities. Does the studio provide coffee and breakfast items, such as muffins and bagels, or snack items such as chips and pretzels? Will the studio order meals for you and your clients? Many studios will order lunch or dinner meals, but put the cost on the invoice. Is there a quiet space for the client to conduct business or make phone calls?

Know the engineer. If you are doing a commercial session, you need an engineer who can work fast under a great deal of pressure, who is great at problem solving and getting good sounds quickly, who is extremely knowledgeable about many styles, and who is comfortable with the equipment.

Reputation. Using a studio with marquis value can enhance your profile. Big-name studios usually cater to the top clients in their respective fields and as a result are more expensive. Learn where the best studio(s) are, how much they cost, and who the engineers are, and incorporate them into your budget if you can afford it.

Ask around. Experienced studio musicians who make their living day after day in this environment are familiar with the studios that are easy to work in, the engineers who are great to work with, the rooms that sound good, and the facilities that make the high-pressure world of recording more relaxed. Get their input.

PROJECT 8.1. RESEARCH STUDIOS

Visit at least three recording studios in your area that are appropriate for producing the type of music that you create. What do you like about each? What are their limitations? Describe each in detail, and be sure to include their rates.

PROJECT 8.2. EVALUATE YOUR STUDIO

Evaluate your personal work space where you will create music most often. What are its strengths and weaknesses? Do you have good isolation? What's the maximum number of people that you could record simultaneously, there? Do you have a good space for meeting with clients? What kind of projects can you do at your home studio? What types of projects will require an outside studio? How much will using your outside studio cost?

Draft a plan for improving your personal studio. Also, make sure that you have information for at least three local studios that you can use for projects beyond the capabilities of your own studio.

CONCLUSION

Your personal recording studio is the focal point of your business, as a writer/producer/engineer. When you're planning your studio, try to work in a number of professional spaces, and also see if you can visit other writer/producers' studios, to get some ideas.

As you master your craft as an engineer, you will develop a better idea of what you need in your studio. Proceed carefully, and don't overspend.

It can be extremely helpful at the start of your career to engineer other people's projects before you engineer your own. That way, you can develop your engineering skills without having to also be the producer and writer at the same time. Engineering other people's projects allows you to learn the incredible discipline, control, and patience that most great engineers possess, without going through the stress that can come with trying to create or elicit a meaningful performance.

Engineering can be one of the most rewarding areas in the creation of recorded music. Like any other craft, there are moments of inspiration when everything falls into place, and other times when you wonder if your ears were stuffed with cotton when you recorded and mixed. The ultimate goal is to make engineering second nature, so that you can devote most of your time and attention to writing and producing music.

CHAPTER **9**

Tracking and Microphone Technique

RECORDING LIVE PERFORMANCES can be extremely rewarding. It requires a much deeper understanding of sound and recording than what is necessary for MIDI-based recording. It also poses the greatest challenges. The ability to mic an instrument or voice in the best way, get the right levels, and blend all the sounds into a wonderful mix are pursuits that engineers have been striving for ever since Thomas Edison invented the gramophone in 1876.

As an engineer, you will have to be the most "micro" and the most "macro" of listeners, always paying attention to everything all of the time. A lapse in concentration can cost you dearly later on. The good news is that over time you will develop your *peripheral hearing—* your ability to hear all aspects of the recording and production while also focusing on any individual task.

SETUP

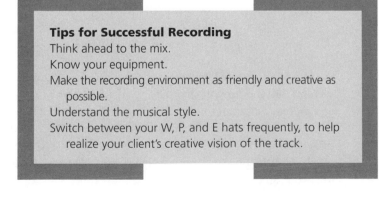

Tips for Successful Recording
Think ahead to the mix.
Know your equipment.
Make the recording environment as friendly and creative as
    possible.
Understand the musical style.
Switch between your W, P, and E hats frequently, to help
    realize your client's creative vision of the track.

Planning ahead for track assignments, musician location in the studio, miking techniques, session protocol, and any special client requirements is fundamental to the success of any recording session.

Keep the microphones you use most commonly always mounted on microphone stands with the cables attached. When the players arrive, it takes only a few minutes to set them up. This allows a session to flow smoothly and more immediately engages the musicians in the recording process. You don't want to be paying musicians to sit while you plug in microphones and figure out cable routing.

ENGINEERING CHECKLIST

Before each recording session, complete this checklist:

Engineering Checklist

O Equipment is well maintained and in good working condition.

O All cables and internal/external connections are functioning.

O Studio and control rooms are clean and tidy.

O Environment is comfortable (e.g., temperature and lighting are appropriate; there are enough chairs).

O Channel assignments are methodical and logical.

O Headphones are set up and functioning.

Here's a suggested method for preparing for a typical tracking session. Say you need to record a song that includes a drum kit, bass guitar, live synth, and vocals. The musicians will be playing along with sequenced tracks of strings, brass, click track (recorded metronome), and percussion. The recording will be done to twenty-four tracks on Pro Tools and, in turn, synchronized to a video display so that you can monitor the visual at the same time.

Before you plug in a single cable, move a fader, or even turn on the equipment, ask yourself: "How am I going to record these instruments?" Ascertain how many tracks you will need for the entire project. The orchestration may call for track assignments such as the following:

TRACK	INSTRUMENT
Tracks 1–7	Drums
	Track 1: Bass drum
	Track 2: Snare
	Track 3: Hi-hat
	Tracks 4 and 5: Toms in stereo
	Track 6 and 7: Overhead microphones for complete drum set
Track 8	Bass guitar direct
Tracks 9–10	Synth in stereo
Track 17	Lead vocal
Track 18–23	Background vocals
Track 24	Click track

A logical layout of tracks on the recording console makes mixing much easier. As your engineering skills increase, you will likely create a layout that works for you. A template, of course, is only a starting point. For example, if I have the tracks available and the drummer has two rack-mount toms and a floor tom, I might be inclined to mic each tom separately and put the bass on track 9.

In the analog world, crosstalk—leakage of audio from one track to another—is a concern. As such, it is best to not record any percussive sound with a large transient (initial attack) on a track next to a quiet sound like an oboe. The percussion track could leak into the oboe track if improperly recorded. Also, in analog recording, try to avoid putting any sounds with loud transient attacks, such as a click track, beside the *SMPTE track* (time code recorded for machine synchronization). The general rule is to not record anything on tracks next to the SMPTE track. In the digital world, there is little concern with crosstalk, so it is not as critical to worry about assigning adjacent tracks to certain instruments.

Write an outline of your track assignments (known as a track sheet), and use it to assign channels before plugging anything in. This way, when you sit down at the console, you just have to turn the faders up and get your levels right away.

It is a good idea to have the main reverb unit patched in and ready to go, including sending it to the headphones, so that when all the levels are set, you can quickly add reverb to the headphones and to the main control-room mix.

MICROPHONE TECHNIQUES

One of the greatest challenges in recording is *miking*—knowing how to mic different instruments and which microphones to use. Be sure to purchase excellent microphone stands and clips. Recordings can be poor because the microphone stand is not holding the microphone firmly, causing the microphone to shift position throughout the session. Also, if the floor of the studio is hollow, the stand will vibrate and transmit the sound into the microphone. Sensitive condenser microphones should be set in a *shock mount*—a holder that is suspended by a non-vibrating, fabric elastic support, which will protect the microphone from picking up any inherent sound transmitted through the stand.

Before you start miking any instruments, determine how much of the natural room sound you want to capture. Decide whether the ambience of the recording space adds to or detracts from the quality of the recording. If it will enhance the sound, experiment with microphone placement. A good benchmark for miking is to imagine where the music you have written would be performed live, in concert.

Conceptualizing the intended ambience of the final mix when you mic instruments will help make the mix session easier. It will be much easier to get the sound you want in the finished product if you begin with a sound that is good. Conversely, if your microphone sounds are not good, the mix can be a nightmare.

Proper miking will help prevent this. As we discussed, different types of microphones have different polar patterns. Learning to use microphones properly requires much trial and error. A particular microphone might sound great on one instrument, but not on another. When you start your microphone collection, be sure that you understand the qualities and best uses of each microphone that you purchase.

AVOIDING PHASE CANCELLATION

When miking a live instrument with more than one microphone, you may encounter a problem called *phase cancellation*. When an acoustic instrument creates sound, it vibrates. The physics of this acoustic phenomenon dictate that when one part of the acoustic surface vibrates up, another part of the surface vibrates down, creating two different points in sound waves—one at the peak of the wave and one at the trough. When these two waves are heard simultaneously in a monaural setting, they cancel each other out, reducing the inherent frequency response or resulting in loss of the sound, particularly in the low frequencies.

We frequently run into this situation when multi-miking certain instruments. The piano is a prime example. It is virtually impossible to mic a piano in stereo without getting some phase cancellation, because it is impossible to find two spots on the soundboard that vibrate in exactly the same way. *Check for phase cancellation with any instrument that you record using more than one microphone, by listening to the combined signal in mono.* If the sound disappears or thins out considerably, relocate the microphones. If the problem is not recognized at recording time, most consoles have a phase-reversal switch, which places a tiny delay in the signal, synchronizing the two signals a little better. You will, in time, learn to recognize phase cancellation quite easily; it sounds as if the recorded sound is being "sucked in," rather than projected out, or like there is a hole in the middle of the sound.

CLOSE MIKING OR DISTANCE MIKING

Microphone use can be organized roughly into two categories: *close miking* and *room* (or "distance") *miking*. If your studio is small and has little natural ambience, you may be more successful using close miking. This way, you can avoid the early reflections and standing waves that easily occur when the microphones are placed somewhere away from the sound source. (*Early reflections* refer to the initial sound reflections from close to the source. *Standing waves* occur when sound reflections combine and increase the apparent volume of that frequency.)

A room with great acoustics can enhance the recording of the instruments. The room creates a much more holistic effect and can add depth and breadth to the sound. It is for this reason that most guitarists prefer having their amplifiers miked rather than going direct. They can "feel" the power of the amplification, which is important to the natural creation of the guitar sound.

Two other terms used in stereo miking are MS (Middle-Sides) and the XY stereo pattern. Each of these can be used to great effect when miking large ensembles from a distance, supported by close miking techniques. They also help in simulating our natural hearing and give a better sense of depth and perception than what we achieve with only close miking.

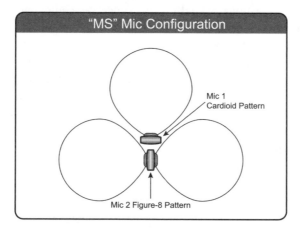

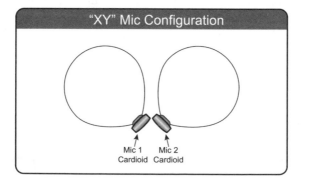

Fig. 9.1. Microphone configurations. (MS = middle/sides)

The MS setup uses two microphones set up right beside each other (see figure 9.1). The first microphone, set to a cardioid pattern, faces the sound source and picks up the sound directly from the front. The second microphone is set to a figure-8 pattern and the sound source. In this way we can duplicate the human sensation of hearing the sound source directly from the front and simultaneously hearing the sound from the right and left sides. This works great for recording horn sections, vocal choruses, or any other "louder" sections.

The XY setup in figure 9.1 uses two microphones in a stereo pair. This time, both microphones are set to a cardioid pattern. They cross over each other at approximately a 90-degree angle and pick up the sound source from the left and right sides respectively. The microphones are exactly the same distance from the players. That way, there is little risk of phase cancellation, as the microphones get the sound waves at the same time. This setup is also very good for duplicating human perception. The two microphones together create the aural image as perceived from one location, much as a set of human ears would hear it.

MIKING INDIVIDUAL INSTRUMENTS

Piano. When recording a grand piano, it is best to mic in stereo. For pop music, place one microphone closer to the keyboard near the low strings, and the other near the high strings to get the attack that will make the piano present in the mix. If there are other performers in the studio, close the piano lid to avoid sound leakage. It is not uncommon for some studios to use PZM microphones fastened to the piano lid so that the lid can be completely closed. (Pressure-zone microphones are omnidirectional microphones affixed to a flat metal plate. They may be fastened to walls, floors, or other surfaces.) For solo pianos, try miking the length of the piano, i.e., the bass strings at the bottom and the high strings towards the front of the piano. If you have enough microphones and the room sounds good enough, mic the room as well. Always check for phase cancellation.

Electric Guitar/Bass. When miking guitar or bass amps, be careful not to use fragile condenser microphones if there is going to be a lot of volume. I have had great success with two or three microphones placed at different areas, particularly close to the speaker grill but slightly off axis of the center of the speaker(s). The Shure SM57 is a dynamic microphone that does a great job on guitar amps, but condenser microphones might also do a good job if the volume is not loud.

Electric basses are sometimes recorded using mics at the amplifier, but often plug direct to the mixing board using a DI (direct-infusion box).

Acoustic Guitar. When miking acoustic guitar, try using two microphones, one near the strings and one near the body of the guitar. Condenser microphones work well in this application. You have to make sure that you find the "sweet spot" on the body of the guitar, an area with an even frequency response throughout the range of the instrument. Some experimentation may be necessary. Asking for help from the guitarist can also be beneficial.

Drums. When miking drums there are many options. I tend to prefer the simpler method, which requires eight or nine (or more) microphones: one microphone per drum, including the bass drum, snare, hi-hat, and toms, and a pair of microphones over the entire kit. It is not uncommon, however, to use two microphones on the snare drum—one on the top head and one on the bottom head by the snares. This will work well on a great-sounding drum, but be careful on a resonant drum with bad hardware and loose snares.

The bass drum has several purposes depending on the style; it should be miked accordingly. If the music dictates that the bass drum be punchy and fat sounding—common in any kind of contemporary pop, funk, r&b, and country music—it's better to place a special microphone, such as an Electrovoice RE20 or AKG D112, inside the bass drum itself. You may have to remove the front head of the drum if the player is not a studio musician. Most studio players are equipped for this. When miking inside of the bass drum, it's common to dampen the head to minimize its vibration and ring. For a jazz tune, the bass drum has a different purpose and is best miked at a distance of about one to two feet from the front head.

If you are recording brushes, it is imperative to mic the snare properly, in order to get all of the nuances of brush playing. The toms are usually miked closely, most commonly with dynamic microphones. The hi-hat usually sounds best with a small condenser microphone in a hyper-cardioid pattern over the far side of the top cymbal.

Save your best pair of condensers to suspend over the kit. You need a pair of microphones that are exactly the same so that the coloration is the same in the stereo field. Choose microphones that are very sensitive to the higher sounds of the cymbals. They could be set in an XY pattern or set apart, but should be in either hyper-cardioid or cardioid, depending on the room. Also, I like to set the frequency filter to roll off as much of the low end as possible. Experiment to find the sounds that most appeal to you.

Vocals. Vocal microphone choices can be as varied as the singers that will use them. Some engineers in the rock field love the way the dynamic microphones sound with their natural compression. The condenser microphones, although not designed for close-range screaming and very loud vocals, can be very effective when placed at a distance from the source. If you are going to need a lot of compression, this might be a good choice, because condenser microphones tend to get a lot more of the middle to high frequencies than dynamic microphones do. I like to start with the AKG 414 for female voices and the Neumann U87 for male voices, and make changes as necessary. If I am not familiar with a particular vocalist, I will ask his or her opinion, or set up two or three microphones to try.

When recording background vocal groups, I have found two ways that work best for me. With only two singers, I have them face each other and set the condenser to a figure-8 pattern. If there is a large ensemble, I usually choose one of two things: have them all gather around one microphone so that they are in eye contact with each other and set the microphone to an omni pattern, or use two microphones in an MS pattern and have them stand in a line. This only works well if the studio has a nice natural ambience. It is good to always use a pop screen of some kind when recording any voice. Pop screens help to prevent plosives—bursts of air that often occur when a vocalist enunciates P, T, K, B, D, and G sounds. If you don't own a pop filter, you can make one by stretching one leg of an old pair of nylons over a coat hanger made into a circle. It doesn't look good, but works great.

Winds. When recording woodwind instruments, the best sound is usually achieved by miking the central area over the keys, about 8 to 12 inches away, but not the end of the bell. If you happen to have the microphones available, you can use a combination of miking the bell and the keys. On brass instruments, place the microphone about 6 to 12 inches away from the bell.

Percussion. Miking percussion can be very tricky. Chances are slim that you will be recording tympani, orchestra bells, and other large percussion instruments in your home studio. However, smaller hand percussion such as shakers, tambourine, congas, and bongos are not uncommon. The condensers work well here and are particularly effective on the metallic sounds. The biggest problem that you can run into is the unusually strong transient, or initial attack, that occurs when you strike an instrument such as tambourine, triangle, or wood block. Because meters cannot react as quickly to these transients, a brief distorted signal can often be recorded and go unnoticed until playback, or at worst, mix time.

Viola and violin. When miking violins and violas, it is wise to record with microphones over the players at a distance of about 2 to 4 feet. If there are two players per stand and the room sounds good, you can use a cardioid pattern. With a larger section of violins and violas, you can suspend the microphone at an even greater distance above the section. In this way you get a wonderful blend of the entire group, while at the same time capturing the performance of several players specifically. Condenser microphones work well on all stringed instruments.

Acoustic bass and cello. When miking a jazz acoustic bass, use a combination of the direct signal from the pickup (if the player has one mounted to the bass) and a microphone wrapped in foam and stuffed inside the bridge to get the intimate sound of the wood and fingers. Condenser microphones work best here.

For both basses and cellos, it is best to set up the microphones in a cardioid pattern about 3 feet in front of the strings. At this distance you can get the richness of the overtones and the blend of the section. Even for solo cello, this setup can work beautifully.

GENERAL MICROPHONE TIPS

Here are a few tips to make your life easier when recording live instruments:

- Know the sounds and characteristics of your microphones.
- Handle all of your microphones with care, especially the fragile condensers and ribbon microphones.
- Keep all of your microphone cables well maintained and make sure the cables are wired correctly so that you don't have electrical phase reversals. Also make sure that they are properly shielded (grounded).
- Avoid overloading the microphone input. Use internal pads (gain-reduction switches) only when necessary. If a sound source is too loud for a particular microphone, use another. If it is really loud, consider a more durable dynamic microphone.

Microphone technique is an art in itself. Mastering it involves an in-depth study of acoustics. If you are not sure about what to do, the musicians most often can offer good advice. As always, using experienced studio players will help you enormously in your recording.

GETTING SOUNDS

Once you have selected and set up the microphones, you have to "get the sounds" for the recording. Here, creativity and engineering come together. My sequence of getting sounds on a recording session with rhythm section and vocals generally is as follows:

STEP 1. Bass drum. Make sure that you are getting a clear and present sound that fits the style of the piece. If the bass drum doesn't have the correct sound, mixing it into the music will be very difficult. It should stand out in a mix without getting in the way of the other instruments. If the drum is too boomy, consider stuffing blankets or other absorbent material into the interior. Also, play around with microphone placement. The closer the microphone is to the beater, the punchier the sound will be. It is also not uncommon to use two microphones on the bass drum, one inside the drum and one close to the beater on the drummer's side.

STEP 2. Snare drum. Many experienced freelance drummers will have a collection of snare drums available and will bring them if you ask. The metal shell drums sound different than wood shells. Also, the deeper the drum, the thicker the sound. Be thinking ahead to the mix and how the presence of the drum will sound in the final mix. I have always liked to use one microphone on the snare, a Shure SM57, set at an angle facing into the drum. If you don't like the sound, try experimenting with different placements. Make sure the microphone is out of the way of the player.

STEP 3. Hi-hat. It is best miked, as are most high-end metallic sounds, with a condenser microphone such as the Neumann KM64. Set to hypercardioid, this microphone does a reasonable job of isolating the hi-hat. Also, you can use EQ and panning to move the perspective of these cymbals around. I like to place the microphone on the far side of and slightly above the top cymbal, facing down. It is also wise to roll off the bottom-end frequencies if you can.

STEP 4. Tom toms. The toms can be tricky to mic. I love the sound of a Shure SM58 on floor toms and the Sennheiser MD421 on the rack toms. But overall, the cheaper dynamics can work very well. You will have to check each drum individually for any ringing overtones or pitches that can be in the way of the clarity. If you hear unwanted ringing or overtones, dampen the drumhead with duct tape or light cloth to eliminate some or all of the ringing. The sound you desire will dictate what is appropriate. After you have the sounds you want for all of the toms individually, have the drummer play fills around them, making sure you have an even balance. If you are bussing all of the toms to two tracks (in stereo), you will have to commit to a stereo perspective at this point, so make sure that you are happy with the panning. I like the standard panning of "drummer's perspective," which is a floor tom on the far right and panning to the far left as tom pitch increases.

STEP 5. Overhead mics. Make sure that you have good microphones for this setup, such as AKG 414s. My favorite setup is to have the microphones separated over different cymbals and facing almost straight down. This gives great stereo isolation, but can present some serious phasing problems. If you do this, it is imperative that you double-check the microphones in mono to listen for any phase cancellation. If it is minimal, it can work great. If not, you might be best served to use the XY setup. Engineers think of the overheads in various ways, but I like to focus on the cymbals.

STEP 6. Refine the balance and blend. After setting all of the proper levels individually and in groups, have the drummer play around the set. Remember that every microphone is open, so you can't assume that the level you had for the snare drum, for example, is going to be just right when the whole kit is playing. Even in the digital world, you are striving for optimum signal-to-noise ratio.

STEP 7. Reverb. Use reverb to set up an ambience that will give the drums (and the drummer) a feeling of space. We will discuss it in depth in a later chapter, but for now, note that it sometimes is a tracking consideration. Use of reverb for monitoring will create a more comfortable sound for the performer. Do *not* put reverb on everything; use it primarily on the snare and toms, with maybe just a touch on hi-hat. On occasion, engineers will add a very slight reverb to the bass drum to give it fullness and a stereo image.

Unless you really have to, do not record the EQ when you are tracking. Rather, save it for the mix (discussed in chapter 11). Once an EQ'd sound has been recorded, it is nearly impossible to recreate the original "dry" sound. EQ is a form of filtering and can have audio distortion attached to it.

STEP 8. Bass. Occasionally, if the piece needs a more dynamic bass sound, you will have to use a compressor for recording. If this is so, use it judiciously and musically. Listen for the low end, but also pay close attention to the low-mid and even high-mid range. You want the bass to cut through the mix without being too loud. If there is a lack of the higher-end frequencies, you will have to boost the bass level to be heard and risk making your mix too bottom heavy and boomy. Also, check for subsonic pitches in the bass, particularly synth bass parts. These can be inaudible on smaller speakers, but can get the speaker cones on larger speakers moving violently, distorting the whole bottom end of the mix.

STEP 9. Guitars and piano. Listen for clarity, warmth, and depth. Even very distorted guitar sounds should have clarity. Ask the guitarists to change their EQ settings on their amps before you add any EQ through the console. Also, you have to determine if you are going to record guitars with effects in stereo, or get those sounds later in the mix. You should have already determined this in your setup process.

STEP 10. Vocals and spoken voice. Listen for clarity, warmth, and sibilance—exaggerated, high frequency components of certain vocal sounds, especially "s" and "sh." Sibilance can be corrected with a de-esser, a compression/EQ combination. Also, listen for popping "p" sounds. The pop filter can take care of this, but you can also try moving the singer slightly off axis.

Also, ask the vocalists to duplicate the dynamic range of their performance as best they can so that you can monitor the level going to tape. If they are very dynamic in their singing, you might consider using compression. If there is any way to avoid this, though, you should. It is a balance between capturing a natural performance, getting a great recording level, and not inhibiting the artist's delivery.

A reminder: it is *critical* to make sure that the singer is comfortable with the headphone mix. When possible, give the vocalist his or her own mix if he or she is singing live with the band. If a singer overdubs at a later time, which is generally the case, this is not an issue. At all times, make sure there is reverb, and EQ the sound to his or her liking, but only for monitoring. Singers who cannot hear themselves well can tire out very quickly or sing out of tune.

STEP 11. Other instruments. Ensure that the sounds of the individual instruments are clear and full. At the same time, be alert for technical problems such as extreme electronic noise, weak levels, phase-cancellation problems, unwanted distortion, inappropriate headphone levels, and routing problems. These should all be worked out before the serious recording begins.

If you maintain your equipment, keep it clean, and are knowledgeable about your system and the signal routing, you shouldn't have any major problems. Once the "red light" goes on, your concern is capturing a performance. Your focus shifts from the technical area back to the creative area. If your setup works, all you essentially have to do is control the transport buttons on your multitrack. You may have to fine tune a little here and there, but you can put your producer's hat back on.

I cannot emphasize enough: always think ahead to the mix. After all the work you have already done, the last thing you want to do is to agonize over a difficult mix. With good sounds, good players, and great writing, your mix should go smoothly.

THE RECORDING PHASE

When you are acting as both the producer and engineer, you have to focus on both the performances and the technical aspects of the recording. It can become very difficult to focus on performance when you are trying to correct technical problems—so get them worked out before you press the Record button. Without your undivided attention to the music, many small issues can slip through the cracks and may be revealed during the mix, when the musicians have gone home.

Two of the great benefits arising from the advent of multitrack recording and the development of the sync head were overdubbing and punching in and out. These advances provided the opportunity to "build" perfect performances, rather than just hoping for the best. There is no doubt that great magic can be captured by a complete performance in one take. But in commercial recording, that is not always the priority, and rarely the reality.

Multitrack recording allows you to do several takes of the same part on different tracks. Then, using the technique of bouncing tracks together, you can compile one good track by using the best parts of each take. This is often referred to as "comping." It involves combining several tracks together to create one mono or stereo track.

PUNCHING IN AND OUT

"Punching" refers to the process of recording small sections over existing, previously recorded tracks. It is used as a way to correct and record over mistakes. To many, the test of skill of an engineer is his/her ability to punch in and out of very tight places in a previously recorded performance, even to the point of recording over a single word or note. Even more precarious can be punching in an entire band in the middle of a song. Every engineer has his or her own style, but here are the considerations that I think make this art work well and avoid creating "the ever-enlarging punch," which occurs when punching in and out erases good material that has to then be rerecorded.

The world of digital recording has lessened, if not eliminated, the necessity for "perfect punches." With nondestructive editing and punches, and the ability to set very specific locations for punching in and out, accuracy is not an issue in most digital software because it is easily attained. However, should you have to work in the tape world, this is a skill you must acquire.

Before you attempt the punch, make sure you know *exactly* when to come in and out. If you are not sure, practice a couple of times. Have a pre-roll of at least several measures and have the player(s) play along with the existing track. This will help get a smooth transition, as the player will have the time and groove going, as well as the phrasing.

I find it very helpful to count the tempo and time to the punch point as if I were playing the recording machine's remote control as a musical instrument. For example, if I know that I want the bass guitar to punch in on beat 4, I will count this: 1-2-3-punch. This is an oversimplification, because on many analog machines, the record circuit relays don't kick in immediately. Thus, when using analog machines, I punch into record mode one sixteenth note before beat 4. This approach works well almost every time. In digital recording, this isn't as critical a problem.

On the punch-out point, I prefer to press Stop rather than Play. The tape machine's relay reacts more quickly to the Stop function than it does when switching from Record to Play.

Avoid punching in during the middle of a breath on a recorded vocal track. This creates a terrible sound and is difficult to fix. It is imperative that you understand the phrasing and performance, including where the performers are breathing before you punch. In the hard-disk recording realm, it is easy to program the in and out punch points on the screen.

Before punching in, ensure that the sound you are recording matches the original take. If you're punching in a vocalist or horn player, make sure they are at exactly the same position relative to the microphone to avoid any apparent level changes or off-axis coloration.

If you have a DAT, leave it running during your session. This monitor mix can be very handy—particularly because it can help you avoid disaster. I once was working on a session in which I played bass. With the band, I recorded a forty-minute track and the band was playing beautifully. When we listened to a playback of the performance, the 2-inch machine was varying in pitch, causing the music to speed up and slow down like a roller coaster. As it turned out, the tape was old and was disintegrating. Nothing could be done and the work was lost. However, the engineer had shown great forethought and had run a DAT recording of the entire session. Fortunately, his monitor mix was so good that with long hours and the use of Pro Tools, he was able to deliver an absolutely incredible recording. All engineers should develop this habit.

Tips for Recording Success

- Keep your equipment well maintained. Test it in advance of your session to confirm that everything is working.
- Take the time required to set up a good monitor mix. The musicians and clients will always appreciate the way it sounds when you listen back.
- Listen at a comfortable monitoring level. This will help you to avoid "burning your ears out," or worse, permanently damaging your hearing.
- Don't erase anything you don't have to. If you can comp tracks, do so instead of punching in and out.
- When recording with analog tape, always record "tails out," meaning, record from inside the roll of tape instead of the end. That is, reverse the take-up and tape reels on the machine, and rewind the tape before starting. This protects your recording by placing the beginning of the music at the hub of the reel. Similarly, store analog tape with "tails out."
- Don't be a button pusher and nervous engineer. Once you are going and everything is working fine, just leave it set. If there is something you need to check on occasion, do so. It is particularly disconcerting to the client to hear you switching speakers, changing levels, checking to monitor the headphone mix, and soloing tracks all of the time. If you need to do something unusual, explain it to the client.
- Be courteous and supportive of all of the performers, no matter how much pressure you may feel.
- Make backup copies of your audio files and mixes!
- Particularly for analog systems, keep meticulous track sheets and session logs, as well as a written record of the microphones, any outboard settings, and EQ settings you use. If you have to go back later and use the same tracks, you will have a good idea of what you did. I like to write the name of the microphone used on every track on the track sheet. Be sure to write down all of the timings you are working with, such as locate points, SMPTE times, and song section times. On your track sheets, write in pencil (things can change), and be as specific as possible in your track descriptions and labels. For example, if you have six vocal tracks, don't just label each one "Vocal." Make sure you differentiate which ones are lead vocals, background vocals, and so on.

PROJECT 9.1. BUILDING RECORDING EXPERIENCE

Develop a plan for gaining experience at recording all different instruments. Periodically, invite musician contacts to your studio, and offer to record them for free, in exchange for their patience as you test different miking techniques. At each such session, plan to record them with at least three different microphones, each in a variety of configurations. Your goal is to develop a feel for the different possibilities with your gear, and to determine whether you need to add to your gear in order to get recordings of appropriate quality.

PROJECT 9.2. MICROPHONE JOURNAL

Create a journal describing microphones. List each mic you own, on its own page (or set of pages). Test that mic in various scenarios, with various instruments, and describe your findings. What is your first choice microphone for all the instruments and voices you commonly record? What do you like for the room? For the drum set overheads? Do they have appropriate accessories, such as pop filters, stands, or booms?

Also test microphones you don't own yourself. Perhaps they are at a different studio, or perhaps a friend or colleague has one you could test. Learn the capabilities of as many microphones as you can, and build an arsenal appropriate to the type of work you do, and to your specific studio.

CONCLUSION

After good musicians, good microphone technique is the most important factor that contributes towards your getting a good recording. Make sure that you have at least one excellent vocal mic and that you know how to use it. Also have microphones for other instruments that you use commonly. Learn their capabilities to the point where you can set up appropriate microphones before your musicians arrive to record. The majority of your testing should be done without the pressure of project deadlines.

CHAPTER **10**

Composing with MIDI

MIDI—SHORT FOR MUSICAL INSTRUMENT DIGITAL INTERFACE—
is a computer protocol that enables instruments, computers, sound
modules, and other devices to communicate. It can allow a computer
to control devices that emit sounds, such as synthesizers and sound
cards.

MIDI and synthesis serve as the most popular and most affordable "orchestra" for current-day recording sessions. MIDI will probably become your main orchestration tool.

The term "sequencing" refers to the process of using a computer-
based (hardware-based) system to input and output MIDI and digital
audio data. MIDI sequencing stores musical information as data;
computers with a MIDI interface can record sounds created by a
"controller," such as a keyboard, and then manipulate the data to create
new sounds. MIDI describes performance information as data organized into a sequence of "events," including note length, pitch, volume,
tone, and other expressive characteristics and effects, such as sustain
on/off, pitch bend, modulation, velocitysensitivity, and glissando.

MIDI sequencers have internal clocks that place any MIDI event
at a specific location in time in the sequence. For example, if your
music were in 4/4, each beat division of that time signature—in this
case, the quarter note—would be divided into equal amounts, determined by the "resolution" of the internal clock. As the MIDI data is
input, the sequencer places that data to the nearest "tick" (1/480 of
a beat) on the internal clock. This kind of detailed resolution allows
for exact note placement. (See also "MIDI Quantizing" on page 136
in this chapter.)

MIDI data moves quickly, doesn't take a lot of storage space, and
is easy to edit. Just as with a word processor (using many of the same
keystrokes), you can cut, paste, move, duplicate, reverse, modulate

(change keys), transpose, and correct timing (quantize) very easily. You also can "humanize" the feel, pan stereo sounds, and use your sequencer in virtually the same way as a recording console. Additionally, MIDI information can be converted into music notation by importing the MIDI data into notation software.

MIDI is also used to control samplers, both onboard the computer and on external hardware machines. The sampler acts as a sound source, with all of the capabilities of MIDI recording discussed above. It translates the MIDI information and plays the actual digital samples with all of the performance features that MIDI has to offer.

Most sequencer programs have the ability to input two types of data: MIDI and digital audio. With MIDI data, you use an input device, usually a piano keyboard, to play the information into the computer. Then you output the MIDI data to a synth/sampler and play your performance with the sound you have chosen. With digital data, you play directly into the sequencer via an analog-to-digital conversion interface, as you would if you were recording to tape. The digital data is stored in audio files and played back by the sequencer.

The most common MIDI controller is a keyboard. Notes are played on the keyboard and transmitted to the computer via a USB, FireWire, or serial port connection. The composer performs notes in real time and MIDI data is transmitted about pitch, volume, duration, and other performance information. Of course, if you are not a strong keyboard player, sequencing can be a frustrating and time-consuming experience. A variety of different manufacturers have attempted to produce powerful MIDI guitars and breath controllers, but they have never had the versatility and capabilities of the MIDI keyboard. For all writers, the piano keyboard has been and will be for years to come the most versatile instrument to use to input MIDI data.

Many programs are available for composing and editing music conforming to the MIDI standard. Some programs, such as Garage-Band and Reason, allow the user to copy and paste prerecorded samples, minimizing the need for developed keyboard skills, but ultimately, writers should be able to play the keyboard competently.

USING MIDI

MIDI tracks are standard in almost every genre of music production today. Many composers writing for live musicians utilize a sequencer, then transcribe the MIDI tracks in order for the live players to perform. This entails a detailed knowledge of the instruments for which you are writing.

When composing with MIDI, think as if you were writing a real score, and write music that is playable by live musicians. You may find it helpful to play each line individually into your sequence. This technique alone will help you determine if the part is playable. If you write in block chords or in step time, you can often create music that is easy for the sequencer to play, but difficult for live musicians.

The MIDI samples that you will use will only sound authentic if you sequence the music realistically. For example, a fretless-bass patch is not going to sound realistic if it is played an octave higher than a real fretless bass. It is also good practice to score out—or at least sketch out—your music, and *then* sequence it. This will ensure that your music sounds as realistic as possible.

MIDI parts will sound most realistic if orchestrated with expression. Include vibrato, slurs, phrasing, dynamics, and other interpretive techniques a performer might use on his or her given instrument. When writing for live players, you indicate many of these elements on the parts; when programming your music on the computer, you add these elements into your sequence to create the feeling and mood of a live performance.

Many years ago, I was the engineer for a writer who was orchestrating MIDI tracks for countless industrial shows. His specialty was writing for full contemporary orchestra. He would come to my studio with his Macintosh SI computer and an early version of Performer. His synths were analog with no digital samples. These were the early days of synchronization between computer and multitrack analog tape, so we would record all of the parts of sequence on several passes, two tracks at a time.

What was amazing was his ability to make these synths sound so realistic. The actual sounds were good, but it was his *writing* that made the tracks work. He played all of the parts in real time, phrased exactly as he had written them, and created wonderful orchestrations. In fact, he would come to the studio with full orchestral scores, as if he had written for an actual orchestra. By the time we mixed, utilizing the appropriate EQ, panning, ambience, and balance to simulate the performance in a studio orchestra, you wouldn't have imagined that this was a sequenced track using synth sounds. It sounded even more amazing over a large PA system.

COMBINING MIDI/AUDIO AND LIVE INSTRUMENTS

A major feature of new sequencing programs is their digital audio capabilities. This allows you to combine MIDI and "real" audio into one sequence, eliminating the need for external multitrack machines.

There are two basic ways to transfer audio into most sequencers. You can record a live performance on a dedicated track. Connect the microphone(s) or patch cable into the audio interface, assign the signal to a specific track, and record. You also can easily import digital audio from any digital source such as DAT machines, CDs, audio files from other programs (some conversions to your file format might be required), and samplers. By using the internal routing, you can place each audio file on dedicated tracks in the sequence and edit at will.

Once digital audio is part of your sequence, you can continue to use the sequencer to create music. You can overdub live instruments on top of your MIDI tracks, import a rough mix off of DAT and sequence a string track on top of it and mix it in, or extract certain parts of a performance that you like and incorporate them into your sequences.

COMPOSITION METHODS

Every writer has a unique process for composing and sequencing. Mine tends to be more traditional. I compose the piece using a real piano, then sequence it. (It is more common these days for writers to compose on a sequencer.) I start sequencing with a basic keyboard track, then add a separate melody track, both recorded in real time. This becomes the "template" for everything else.

Real time is recording an actual performance. **Step time** is the recording of each individual note or chord one by one, at specific locations that you select. As a rule, real time gives a musically accurate performance with feeling and expression. Step time is used most often by people with limited keyboard skills, and can sometimes give a stiff and nonmusical performance that lacks phrasing and expression.

To overcome a rigid performance, you have to add the phrasing and dynamics that would exist in a real performance. Solo each part as you work on the sequence, and listen critically to determine if the sound and approach are musical. Listen to certain tracks with a metronome, and make timing corrections by using the editing functions. Then, put all the tracks together and listen for any irregularities that detract from the feel or sound.

The pitch and modulation (mod) wheels on the controlling keyboard are very useful in editing in real time. By thinking ahead to the mix as you are working, you can envision the tracks placed in their appropriate ambience and edit accordingly.

First, I program the drums in much the same way as recording onto the multitrack—bass drum on track 1, snare on 2, etc. This provides great editing control in the mix. With sequencers as powerful as they are, you will have unlimited MIDI tracks and mix capabilities, so there is no reason to conserve tracks. Also, using many tracks makes it easier to play fills and individual voices, and then work with them afterwards.

After the drums, I sequence the bass track. This adds the bottom end and gives the harmonic and rhythmic foundation for the groove. At this point, I will have a good idea of the framework and continuity of the piece, can make any musical changes without investing too much time and effort, and continue to orchestrate from there.

As I build the sequence, I listen to the parts individually and in different combinations to make sure they work together. A tom fill that is off by a few "clicks" will sound unnatural and affect the whole groove. Or, if the bass part is not "in the pocket" with the snare and bass drum, the groove will suffer. Everything has to work together as it does in live performance.

This becomes even more important if you are using MIDI rhythm tracks for live players to play over. For example, if a sequenced guitar part doesn't sit in the groove, even to the slightest degree, the soloists will have difficulty locking to that track.

As the piece develops, I layer the parts over each other and make revisions as necessary. Keeping each instrument or part on separate tracks gives more control. As I work, I write all patch names and settings in the notes column for each track. Should the patches get lost, I can easily reset. If I do any internal editing within the hardware synthesizer itself, I save these settings as system-exclusive (sysex) settings via MIDI. Therefore, every time I start the sequence, all of my settings within the synth are reset to my chosen parameters. Of course, with the newer soft synths, these settings are easily saved within the software itself, making the sysex settings unnecessary.

MIDI QUANTIZING

One of the more powerful tools of a MIDI sequencer is its ability to quantize—alter the attack and release times of any MIDI event, such as notes, note length, pitch bend, modulation effects, velocities, etc. to align with a particular tempo. This creates a more rhythmically correct performance. In addition to quantizing notes, you can also quantize things like patch changes and mod-wheel and pitch-wheel settings.

Quantizing places MIDI events in exact time locations that you specify. Events are aligned to a grid based on the settings you choose and on the internal clock. Typically, you can quantize in divisions of note length as short as a 1/128th note and as long as eight beats. A popular approach is to quantize to the next shortest note that is in the music. For example, if the shortest note is a 16th note, I try quantizing to 32nd notes. This will correct most, if not all, timing problems.

Set quantization parameters with care. Overquantizing can create a very stiff and grooveless track. Occasionally, a machine-like, overquantized character is desired, such as in techno music, but in most writing and recording, you will be aspiring to produce smooth, flowing, and natural-sounding tracks.

Quantizing risks losing some of the feel of a real-time performance. If not done properly, quantizing will clip notes, eliminate attacks, change velocities, and occasionally make your track unmusical. All good sequencers possess a "preview" feature, which quantizes the track as you listen, but without writing permanent changes to the sequence. Use the preview feature often, and don't commit to the quantizing until you are convinced the sound is going to work.

Because severe quantizing can create the same rigid effect as step-time input, it is often better to correct individual notes in order to maintain the original feel of the performance. In this way, you maintain the integrity of the original performance but eliminate the obvious flaws. This benefits your track, but can be time consuming. Also, setting the quantization parameters such as quantize sensitivity, swing, and note subdivision size (clock divisions) helps maintain the feel of the music.

MIDI EDITING

All sequencing software has several ways to edit: event list, graphic event, and notation. The Event List mode includes a window that displays every MIDI event in chronological order by measure number, beat number, and clock division (tick). This window exists on all sequencing programs. The event-list window numerically displays several events affecting each note, on one line: measure number, beat number, and ticks; type of event; exact pitch; note-on and note-off velocity; and note length.

In Digital Performer, each quarter note is divided into 480 ticks. Hence, a MIDI event at measure 1, beat 2, second eighth note would show in the event list window as 1|2|240.

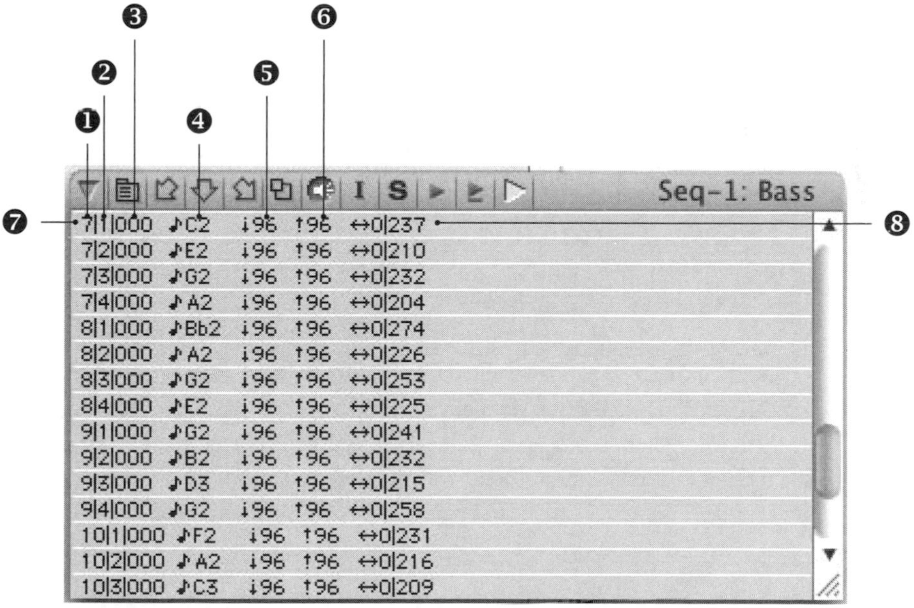

① Bar
② Beat
③ Tick (beat subdivision: 480 ticks = 1 beat)
④ MIDI Note Name/Pitch. In this case, C2.
⑤ Note-On Velocity (0 to 127, where 0 is no attack and 127 is hardest attack). 96 is medium hard.
⑥ Note-Off Velocity (0 to 127)
⑦ Note On. These notes all begin exactly on the beat. 7|1|000 means bar 7, beat 1, exactly on the beat, with no extra ticks (000/480).
⑧ Note Length. These notes all last about an eighth note. 0|237 means 0 beats plus

Fig. 10.1. Event List editing window

If the entry is a note event, it will show an eighth note and then the exact pitch, such as A4. If the entry is a chord, several notes would appear occurring on or, more likely, near the same time, but with each note on an individual line. The note-on and note-off velocity is next, indicated by up and down arrows, followed by note length. In this window, you can also choose to display the MIDI events in real time (or clock time, as is done on multitrack locators), or in SMPTE time, consisting of hours|minutes|seconds|frames.

Another editing window is the graphic-event window. It displays all MIDI events in two areas: the "piano roll" and the event editor window. The piano roll displays note information, including pitch, as represented by a keyboard on the left-hand side of the piano roll, and note length, as indicated by the size of the "strip." All of these parameters are easily changed using functions such as click and drag, and cut and paste. One benefit of this window is the pencil tool feature, with which you can draw in MIDI controller events such as volumes, velocities, panning, mutes, and sustain.

The third editing window is the notation window. This is an excellent tool for writers, as it displays MIDI note information on specific staves, allowing the user to cut and paste sections, drag notes to different pitches, correct voicings, and add notes of a specific length to the music.

Once the music is programmed and the editing is done, you should have a solid performance. If necessary, you can fine-tune the sequence, enhance the feel, pan tracks, balance the levels, and mix via the mix console. Most MIDI software allows you to automate all the settings, including volume, plug-ins, mutes, panning, effects routing, and EQ, creating an environment that gives complete control of the mix at any time. This enables changes to be made almost instantaneously.

INDUSTRY SPOTLIGHT: SYNCHRONIZATION

Synchronization methods have been necessary in film production ever since the advent of the "talking picture." When motion pictures and television shows were made using film, the actor's dialog, narration, additional sound effects, and music were *not* recorded onto the film in the camera, but onto separate recorders. As different scenes were shot, the photography crew captured the visual elements, while the sound crew recorded the dialog on separate audio tape. After the movie was completed and rough edits were made, the music and sound effects were recorded onto yet another tape, which would then have to be synchronized with the film, and finally mixed together by the postproduction engineer(s).

In the 1950s, the Society of Motion Picture and Television Engineers (SMPTE) incorporated a military code into a format called SMPTE that identified every frame of a motion picture by indicating the hour, minute, second, and frame. In this way, each frame of a motion picture could be uniquely identified in a numerical way, with each second being divided into a certain number of frames. There are several different frame rates that include:

- 24 fps (frames per second) used for motion picture work
- 25 fps EBU standard for European television
- 29.97 fps NTSC standard for North American color videotape
- 30 fps NTSC standard for North American black and white videotape

Today, it is possible to have several programs running at once, all synchronized with time code. You can have a video program running in sync with your sequencer without having to use any external hardware. In this way, anyone that has that software and knows how to use it can write music to visuals.

One other type of time code is the MIDI Time Code, or MTC. MTC is the MIDI equivalent of SMPTE time code. All devices that use MTC have built-in converters that will convert the SMPTE to MTC, enabling these devices to work together.

Another important development is MIDI Machine Control, or MMC. This allows sequencing programs to act as the master machine for any number of external hardware devices that also use MMC. The primary difference between MMC and SMPTE/MTC is that MMC is usually transmitted and received via MIDI cables, rather than the standard 1/4-inch, TT, or XLR cables used for SMPTE. Communicated as system-exclusive messages, the commands are sent to the hardware via the MIDI interface and returned via MIDI in and out. If the machines use SMPTE, another interface has to be used to convert the SMPTE to MIDI Time Code to be returned to the sequencer. This MMC/MTC synchronization code works well with the new generation of multitrack units, such as the new series of all-in-one workstations.

To prepare for synchronization, be sure that you include both SMPTE and a click track in your recording. Verify that your SMPTE frame rate is consistent on all devices, including sequencing software, all digital tapes (with the exception of DAT, which *usually* doesn't have a SMPTE track), digital audio and video software programs, and videos.

Always include at least a two-measure count-in, either with a click track or a recorded countoff by one of the musicians. Without a countoff or warning clicks, adding a live instrument or vocal accurately to the beginning of the track is nearly impossible.

PROJECT 10.1. MIDI INVENTORY

These tasks will help you to use your MIDI setup efficiently and keep your inventory of MIDI sounds fresh.

1. What MIDI gear do you have? What MIDI software is on your computer? List all your MIDI-compatible items. Are you getting the most out of your existing MIDI programs? Can you access all your MIDI sounds through all your sequencers? If not, develop a plan for becoming more proficient at MIDI.

2. What are your favorite MIDI sounds? If you haven't already, organize them into templates for some of the standard MIDI ensembles you do, such as rhythm sections in various styles. Make it easy to immediately begin sequencing, without having to hunt for the right sounds.

3. Search the Internet for free MIDI sound libraries, and make this a habit at least every few months. Ask other writer/producers you know what freeware MIDI sound sources they are using, and point them to the sources you have found yourself.

CONCLUSION

Depending on the type of work, much of your recording and mixing could be focused on MIDI-controlled synths and samplers, which present advantages and disadvantages. Certain problems inherent in live recording don't exist to the same degree in the MIDI realm. However, MIDI sounds can be very artificial and difficult to place in a mix. Also, samples and synthetic sounds can contain extraneous overtones, effects, or preset stereo placements that clash with other instruments. Your ears have to be attuned to all of these things.

CHAPTER 11

Mixing

WHEN THE RECORDING SESSIONS ARE COMPLETED, you are ready to move to the next phase: mixing. Mixing is the art of combining all of the final tracks into a stereo image (or quadraphonic, 5.1 surround sound, 7.1 surround sound, or others, depending on the project). This can be the most challenging of all the production phases, because it has such finality. All of your effects choices—balances, panning, EQ, ambience, special effects—will define the mix.

When mixing, you need to have clear concepts of the style, sound, balance, and soundscape before you begin. During the mix process, expand and experiment as you see fit, but make sure to accomplish these objectives.

The mixes should be a good sonic representation of the musical style and work well for the intended medium (i.e., album, film/TV, jingle, and so on). They should be well balanced, clear, and sound good in a variety of settings and on different speakers.

During your mix, stay as close as possible to the aural soundscape you are emulating. You need a clear concept of the ambient effects that you will use, balances of the instruments and voices (where used), special EQ settings, dynamic effects, as well as other factors. If needed, bring a reference recording to the mix that closely resembles the sound you are trying to achieve.

Verify that the mixes will work well for the format on which they will likely be played (i.e., television, radio, computer system, CD player, and so on). Most outside studios will have a variety of speaker systems that duplicate every situation, from the most advanced audiophile systems to the cheapest television and radio speakers. Always monitor and check your mixes through various speakers. Make sure that the important elements aren't lost. These include the voiceover, solos, any sounds that are written with direct relationship to events on picture, and vocal melodies. For example, if the piece is a groove tune, confirm that the bass/drum combination is kicking underneath the track and that everything is grooving on top.

When you have finished mixing, stand outside the control room or away from the console and listen casually. This can supply a good representative idea of how a listener would perceive your mixes. Use your "peripheral hearing" to make sure that all of the orchestration elements work well together and don't crowd the mix.

Ensure that the focal point of your track is present and that the *message* of the music is clear. I have always viewed mixing as a powerful means of orchestration. Mute parts that aren't working, strengthen weaker parts by using certain outboard effects, and make sure the feel and groove are as strong as needed. Your mix should consistently maintain sonic clarity.

If your composition was written to picture, play your mixes along with the video. Make any improvements to the mixes that would better support the visual. Be certain that the effects don't get lost on small speakers and that the reverb is present where needed.

OVERVIEW

When you're mixing, your task mostly concerns combining sounds together after live sounds are recorded, MIDI instruments are sequenced, and samples/loops are assembled.

Mixing and sound imaging are like painting, and as a mix engineer, you need to think about what perspective will best suit the music. Every mix has a focal point, just like every painting has a focal point.

In my mixing classes, I like to examine da Vinci's "Mona Lisa." I ask my students, what's the focal point and what's the background? As Leonardo da Vinci set it, the subject is set against a background with trees, a stream, and a little pathway leading down to the water. It's like a standard mix, with the vocals being up front, and supported by the rhythm section.

Fig. 11.1. "Mona Lisa," by Leonardo da Vinci

But what if she was smaller in relationship to the background? That would be like a heavy metal mix, where the vocals are set a bit buried, and the background is more prominent.

Let's get more "Monty Python" about it. What if we put her exactly as she is but placed her in front of the Empire State Building? What if we put her in a soccer game? Would it have the same impact? It's like changing the groove. Or what if her face took up the whole painting, with just a little background behind her, like a close-up? Could that be a better setting, for some commercial purpose—selling lipstick, perhaps?

By changing the perspective, the whole experience becomes different. When the ambience changes, the subject is perceived differently. When you're the writer, producer, and engineer, you can explore many possibilities for what the subject of a mix should be and how you might control it.

BALANCE AND PANNING

The two most critical controls in mixing are volume and panning. We have already mentioned these, in the context of mixing boards, but let's define precisely what they do and how they are used.

Balance is the relative volume (level) of the sounds in relationship to each other.

Panning is how the sounds are set in the stereo field: left, center, or right, or some variation in between (e.g., slightly left of center).

These contribute most profoundly to the sense of perspective. Generally, volume and panning get set first, and then other tools are applied.

Balance and panning are the most rudimentary controls, but they also are among the most critical to get right. They set the most essential aspects of the imaging and perspective—whether Mona Lisa is so close you can just see her smile, so far back that she's just coming out of the water, or framed as we generally see her.

It's hard to say that there's a right or wrong way to set the perspective, though few would argue with Da Vinci's choice, from a purely aesthetic viewpoint. Different perspectives will achieve different results, though. If the painting's purpose was to advertise the park in the background, the client might suggest a change.

The task is to determine the most important focus. What's the main subject, and what's supporting that, in the background? What perspective would suit the music best? These controls will help to frame the center of interest. They are at the heart of mixing.

A mix in the style of heavier bands, such as Lincoln Park or Disturbed, would not work as well for singers such as Toni Braxton, Whitney Houston, or Mariah Carey. Mixes of harder music, starting with Led Zeppelin, set vocals farther back, which emphasized the power of the sound around them. On the other hand, Toni Braxton's beautiful voice (listen to "Unbreak My Heart") is more intimate. Her voice is closer upfront and intimate in the mix, which tells a different story, sonically—expressing a feeling of emotion and pain. It's not that one is good and the other is bad. They simply serve different purposes.

So, set the volume and panning first, to clarify the main focus.

TYPES OF SOUND MODIFIERS

Once the balance and panning are set, you can work with sound modification tools to create the mix's ambience.

Sound modifiers may be applied from within a computer program or mixing board, or they may reside in *outboard units*—hardware units dedicated to each purpose. Most commonly for computer use, they will be plug-ins in a software mixer channel.

Three sound modifiers are most critical: EQ, compression, and reverb. Devices that control these three exist in hardware and software forms, as do many timbre manipulation devices. We will discuss them in more detail in chapter 12, but here are basic descriptions.

EQ is short for equalization. An EQ unit controls the frequency spectrum of a sound, and which low or high frequency harmonics are emphasized. By using EQ to isolate the frequency spectrum of each sound in a mix, and carefully controlling redundancy of these frequencies, a clear, powerful mix is achieved, with minimum muddiness.

Compression evens out the relative loud and soft parts of a track, making it seem smoother, and allowing the overall volume to increase without *clipping* (distorting). They are especially common on bass tracks and vocals, or on an overall mix, to add punch or power.

Reverberation (or just "reverb") gives the sound a sense of space, and broadens the stereo field.

Those three are most critical, but there are thousands more sound modifiers (and counting!), and many can improve your recordings greatly. We will discuss many of them in the next chapter.

AUTOMATION

The mixing process begins with a *rough mix*. This is a set of initial volume and panning settings that sound pretty good. But mixing is a dynamic process. Levels change over time. You might want different relative volumes at different points of the mix. For example, if a song has an instrumental beginning, a saxophone melody might have a higher level at the intro, and then be set farther back in the mix once the lead vocals enter.

In the above example, the engineer would physically move the sax-level *fader* (switch) down, after the intro, and make dozens or hundreds of similar corrections, behaving almost like another performer, in creating a live performance. The musical needs might require a "four-hand mix," with two engineers simultaneously changing controls, as the music was recorded into a more final form. You had to learn the moves. It was like choreography, and it required practice, many hours of work, and long lists of the necessary modifications.

Automation technology made this much easier. We can now record such changes, as we go. After parameters are recorded, the automation controls repeat the changes to the controls. Recording consoles typically automate only volume and mute controls. Software tools can automate every single setting of every type of unit, which makes them extremely powerful and precise. In a software tool, for example, you can automatically change the amount of depth of reverberation that occurs over the course of a track. It's a lot of control, and the machine does all the work.

I still do make some lists, though. When I am mixing, I'll often just listen and make notes, and not change any controls. I'll write, "Vocals too quiet at bar 5, the hi-hat needs to be to the left." Then I'll make the changes and listen again. I'll listen from behind the console, in the beginning. Getting closer to final mix, I'll wander around the room. I might even go into the hallway, and listen. I'll take my notebook, leave the room with the door open, and look at bulletin boards, drink coffee, and make notes. This separates me from the fixation of the studio, so that I can concentrate on how the mix really sounds. I can then go back to the studio, automate the changes, and listen again. (For this reason alone, automation tools are greatly liberating.)

In this regard, these software tools are enormously flexible and easy to use. That's one of the benefits of the software environment. Hardware consoles may cost a thousand times more than the software, but the software can accomplish so much more, in terms of automation.

But all media, including computers, have limitations. Perhaps hardware systems have more limitations than software, at this point in history, but not everyone agrees that software-based systems are superior.

Does this increased automation control make for better music? It's like autopilot on airplanes. Does it make for a safer pilot or a lazy pilot? If they were to get into trouble, could they really fly the airplane?

PROCESS

It's hard to be dogmatic, when teaching about the mixing process, as everyone finds their own style. I'll present a basic approach. In practice, it's not a straight line, and I'll do a bit of one thing, move to something else, back to the first thing, and so on, continually refining the mix as I go. But here are my basic steps:

1. Balance and Panning
2. Reverb and Dynamics
3. EQ

My first step is to set the starting panning and balance levels of each part. Begin by getting a rough idea of the proper perspective and place of each track. Set initial volume relationships, and start the stereo imaging process. It's rough sanding, at this stage. Lay out the stereo image, and find a unique space for each part.

Then, automate how the basic settings will change, over the course of the mix. Determine what the main focal point of the mix should be at each moment—whether the focus is the vocals, lead instrument, or something else. The focal part needs space to stand out, but it does not necessarily have to be significantly louder than the other parts. It never works to just use volume to frame a part. Panning, EQ, and other tools also help to draw focus.

When one part comes up, other parts need to go down. Everything has a relationship in mixing. That's what makes it such an art.

After levels and panning are set, work on the ambience, using reverb. In computer-based systems, a good reverb is processor intensive, and so I find it best to use one reverb device for all the main parts. This also gives a uniform sound, as if all the parts are sounding in the same space. Create the ambience and feel—the image and space.

After reverb, add dynamics processing: compression, gates, and so on. This step will help to unify the mix, eliminate background noise, and smooth out any dynamic variations.

Finally, add EQ at the end. EQ is a refining tool and helps the parts sound clear and separate. It is important for imaging and placing parts in the 3D landscape of sound. By adjusting EQ, you can tweak good sounds to fit in better with the rest of the band.

Listen like an engineer, not like a musician, when you're mixing. Musicians listen aesthetically. Music is an emotional experience, for performers. They will appreciate finer musical points, such as harmony and the lyrics' dramatic meaning, focusing on the feelings being expressed.

The engineer focuses on sound. This is challenging for writers, but to create an optimal product, you need to give the sound appropriate attention. The sound must be informed by the music, but it needs its own attention. You must separate yourself from the emotional experience of the music, even though you wrote it for emotional reasons, such as Dr. Scholl's insoles. But there is an emotion to that, which the music must articulate. Like painting, the task is to set each element and color in the best place to deliver the message.

REFERENCE RECORDINGS

When you're mixing, keep a great recording in the same style close at hand, and use it for a reference. Our ears are very deceptive, and they can fool you into believing that something sounds good, when in fact, it doesn't. As our eyes can become accustomed to the dark, our ears too can become accustomed to the dark—the darkness of a crappy mix. Having that "light" reference can keep your focus.

We learn music by imitating artists we admire. Mixing is no different. If I took a song, say "Norwegian Wood," copied it, and called it "Canadian Wood," I'd be in a lot of trouble very quickly. But there are no such copyright restrictions on mixes. As an engineer, you can use the same instruments, levels, panning, effects, and so on, from another recording, and recreate something of its sound. This is legal, and it's an excellent way to learn.

To this day, I copy mixes. I've been mixing a jazz album, lately. The whole time I'm mixing, I've got a CD reference handy that's in the same style. I really love the sound of this recording, and I am not ashamed to say it. I constantly A/B them, listening to my mix and then the reference CD, and I try to get as close as I can to it, at least, as my starting point.

In the end, I'll get a good mix. Nobody will ever guess what I'm using as my model because it's different music.

ENGINEERING YOUR SOUNDSCAPE: HEARING IN THREE DIMENSIONS

I had the opportunity to work often at Grant Avenue Studios, the studio in Hamilton, Ontario, Canada that was owned by the great producer Daniel Lanois (Peter Gabriel, U2, Bob Dylan) and his brother Bob Lanois. Daniel was working closely with Brian Eno, the great English producer and master of "soundscapes." It was during this period that I learned to think of sound in three dimensions: depth, panning, and layering from top to bottom. The concepts of depth and panning were easy to imagine, as they are controlled to a great extent by relative level, ambience, and the pan pots on the console. But layering the image from top to bottom was difficult to grasp, as there wasn't a specific dial or knob to do that. This is where the phenomenon of "psychoacoustics" comes into play. Our ears perceive low frequencies at the bottom and high frequencies at the top of the aural landscape.

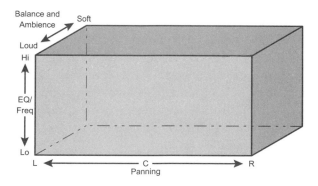

Fig. 11.2. 3D Aural soundscape

To understand the full spectrum of the three dimensions, you have to "stare" between the stereo speakers as if there is a "painting" of sound in front of you. By focusing on the music in this way, you can virtually "see" the aural image in front of you. At the console, you are the artist who creates this image.

One of the interesting elements of this concept is how the relative balance of an instrument or voice changes through EQ and panning. For example, if there is a guitar track with very little mid-range EQ panned in the center with the lead vocal, these two sounds will tend to work against each other, making it difficult to clearly hear each. However, panning the guitar slightly to the side increases its presence. The more you pan, the more present the guitar becomes without you ever having to touch the fader to make it louder. EQ can also generate the same result in "apparent" level changes. In this example, by adding a little top end, the guitar appears to be louder without changing any levels.

It is usually best to reserve most of the use of EQ until the mix phase. EQ helps blend all of the elements of a piece together into a beautiful soundscape; it shouldn't necessarily be used to change the natural sounds of the instruments. When working with individual tracks in the recording process, engineers typically make some initial, minor EQ adjustments to correct some problems, but save most of the equalization until working with the entire mix. This way, EQ can be applied in the full mix to bring specific frequencies more perspective.

FINE-TUNING

When the rough mix is set, it's time to go into more detail. Now, it's time to learn the performances intimately. To start, go through each track and, using automation, mute the areas of the piece where the artist is not performing. This greatly reduces the risk of unwanted sounds in the mix, such as breathing, amp noise, and even squeaky chairs. When muting tracks, make sure that you don't mute before the audio has completely finished.

After that, work on the tracks individually. Solo each track and use basic EQ to get close to the projected desired sound. Don't spend a lot of time on this, since most of the fine-tuning of EQ will occur when all of the tracks are playing together. For example, you could spend much time EQing, compressing, and gating two guitar tracks, only to find that when you put the tracks together, they are horribly out of tune. (Of course, this most likely would have been addressed in the recording phase.)

Again, use your reference CD containing a mix similar to the style you are working on. I put the reference song in repeat mode and let it run for the *entire* mix session. If I am losing focus, my ears are getting tired, or I just need to hear something different, I monitor the CD. It is a great point of reference and a wonderful way to learn.

FADER PLACEMENT

An important technical area of mixing is fader placement. The optimum level for signal-to-noise is to have the fader at around the zero mark (unity gain). However, as a general rule, be sure to always leave enough headroom to make needed increases. Start with the faders around the midpoint as you get sounds in the mix, and use the trim adjustment (if it is present) to make any minor increases or decreases. If all of the faders are up full and you have not added in several tracks, you will constantly be resetting levels and relative balances.

CASE STUDY: APPROACHING A MIX

Here's an example of how to approach the mix of a pop tune for broadcast with a band consisting of drum kit, bass guitar, electric guitar, piano, synth, and vocals.

Begin with the bass drum. Adjust the level, add any appropriate or desired EQ and effects, and check the panning to obtain a good sound. Then do the same for snare, hi-hat, toms, and finally overheads. Next, listen to the whole drum kit and set a good relative balance and panning. I was once told that you can't have enough snare drum and bass drum in a final mix, and, although that is an exaggeration, you don't have to be timid about "feeling" these instruments in the mix; as a rule, you shouldn't have to struggle to hear them. The snare or bass drum is not going to drown out the lead vocal, unless it is at an unreasonable level. Don't be afraid to let the track "groove." If the style of music permits and you're looking for a "tighter" sound from the drums, gate the snare and toms. I would also boost the very high end (about 8 to 12 kHz) on the cymbals to add "air" to the sound.

Now, add the bass guitar and make sure that it works and blends well with the drum kit. This forms the bottom of the mix to a great extent, and usually, the heart of the groove. It has to be tight and solid, regardless of style. Subtle use of compression on the bass can often help. It can smooth out big dynamic range differences (particularly with the slapping style), and you can give the perception of a more sustained and fatter sound.

Solo the bass guitar and bass drum to make certain they work together and complement each other in groove and sound. The bass drum adds the attack to the bass guitar notes and conversely, the bass guitar gives length to the bass drum's lack of sustain. At this point, and if possible, I often subgroup the drums to one fader. This will not sacrifice the individual control, but will give more control of overall balance.

Next, add the guitar, piano, and synthesizer. Instruments such as guitar and piano usually should be very present in the mix. Your musical taste ultimately determines their balance, sound, placement, and EQ. Find a good place in the stereo field to allow the main guitar and keyboard parts to stand out without getting in the way of the heart of the song. Synthesizers, especially padding sounds, sound very good when they are mixed slightly back, panned over the stereo field with a little high end. In this way, you can create a blanket for a vocal or lead instrument to float over.

When the focal point of the writing is the vocal, take special care to preserve the performance integrity, while at the same time make it work within the mix. In pop record production, I like to break vocal mixing into two types: the vocal that is "handed" to you and the vocal that you have to go "into" the music to get. Some vocals are just handed to us and we don't have to work hard to hear them. A common example is vocals in adult-contemporary pop production. These vocals usually sit on top of lush bed tracks, are easy to distinguish, and don't require a lot of listening effort. This makes it easy to hear all the parts and requires less of the listener.

In harder, heavier music, vocals are often placed a little back in the mix. This forces the listeners to dig into the music and concentrate in order to hear the lyrics and performance. Listeners are then psychologically surrounded by the music—an outstanding effect. When we hear a vocal track, our ears naturally focus on that sound, much like our eyes are drawn to the focal point of a painting.

Whenever you are in doubt, use the CD that you have running in the background to refresh you regarding good relative level and sound. When you are mixing, ask yourself, "What is the purpose of this part in the track?" Every part has its place and all should center around and support the lead "voice." Occasionally, you will have to mix some of your favorite parts into the background for the greater good of the mix.

AMBIENCE IN THE MIX

Determine the feeling you want the music to convey and use effects to create it. Generally, the longer and deeper the reverb, the more distant or floating the performance will sound. If you want to have an intimate, in-your-face sound, use very short reverbs. Conversely, a lush sound can be created with longer reverbs. Be careful of the instruments on which you use reverb. Extremely low- and high-pitched instruments can be very problematic. By listening objectively throughout the mix, you can determine if the ambience is correct.

Make sure that the reverbs, choruses, delays, flangers, and other effects you use do not take away from the clarity of the mix. Adding too much reverb on the hi-hat, for example, can create a lot of high-frequency "noise" that results in unwelcome hiss on the overall mix. Similarly, too much reverb on the bottom end can really muddy up the mix. Monitor the reverb return as the mix progresses; an auxiliary send can be turned up mistakenly and unwittingly sent to the reverb, creating distortion. If possible, also solo the aux send to confirm which instruments are feeding into the device associated with that send. Your mixes could lose clarity because of small, unintended actions like these.

MONITORING THE MIX

Get into the habit of monitoring your mixes at different levels and on different speakers. Monitoring at very low levels can be very revealing in terms of balance and EQ. It can be helpful to step out of the control room, leave the door open, and listen from just outside. This will help you to be more objective, and prevent you from fixating on details. You can get the feeling of how the mix "moves the air" and how its elements work together from a different perspective. Listening at a louder level can reveal low-frequency problems that might otherwise go unheard. Monitoring the mix briefly in mono is very important as it can reveal phasing problems. As a final check, listen on headphones for better delineation of panning, balance, extraneous noise, and equal weighting between left and right sides.

Listen to the recording through an average television set or home stereo system. Make a CD of the final mix and listen to it on a typical car stereo system. If the mix sounds good both in the studio and in the car, your mix is complete. If it doesn't, write some notes about the problems. Make those changes, and check again. You will get a good mix quickly this way.

DELIVERING THE FINAL PRODUCT

With technology changing so quickly, the final product can be delivered in a variety of digital formats. Many clients will even request delivery of the final product over the Internet. Be clear on what the client needs. Do they need a particular set of timings, SMPTE offsets, mixes labeled in a particular manner, mixes at specific sample rates, cues in a certain order, a stereo mix, or a multitrack Pro Tools file? In your contract, specify when, where, in what format(s), and to whom the final product is to be delivered. You can also specify whether the completed projected is to be mailed, sent by courier, hand delivered by you, or otherwise.

If you are making a record, most often you will deliver a CD-R copy of the mixes, either as audio or data. Additionally, stereo analog mixes are still quite common. This will go either to the record label for the mixes to be approved and subsequently mastered, or if the record label is pleased with the mixes and sequence of songs, it will be delivered directly to the mastering studio. *Mastering* is the process of adjusting all tracks of a recording to be consistent in level and sound. It is a specialized skill, and you should hire a mastering engineer for this stage, if you are producing an album.

Film and television use several formats. For smaller projects such as jingles, underscoring, and other television and radio work, CD-R is most common. However, other formats are being requested more frequently. As there is often a postproduction process—blending of visuals, dialog, sound effects, and music—you may be called on to supply a variety of formats. Most television work still uses stereo mixes. However, with the advent of surround sound in theatres and the proliferation of DVD players and surround-sound systems in the home, it is not uncommon to either deliver the final product in a format to be mixed at postproduction (for example, Pro Tools multitrack versions) or in audio surround sound that you mix yourself. You might be called upon to mix your own music with the film director and music supervisor present.

However you deliver your music, your final product should look great. Make sure the packaging is professional and that all CD, DAT, cassette, and disk cases and jackets are *neatly* labeled. Go the extra mile by personalizing the package. On several occasions, I made copies of the music scores I had written, had them bound in a nice booklet with a colorful cover, and gave that to the client as a gift. This kind of gesture is always received warmly.

TEN MIXING TIPS

Here are ten tips for mixing commercial music.

1. Keep lead vocals prominent and clear, especially if the words are selling a product.
2. Test your mix in mono and on cheap speakers. People will listen through the speakers on their TV sets, portable radios, and computers. Your mixes must work well in all of these. A tip is to double the bass up an octave, when this is a particular danger. That way, if the speaker can't handle the low frequency, at least the bass part will be heard.
3. Take a break. Our ears can get tired after listening at loud levels, so I listen at medium levels.
4. Check the mix at all different volume levels. Our ears don't have a flat response at different volume levels. We lose detail

at the low end, when the volume is too soft. Mostly, listen at the volume that listeners do.

5. A good mix takes time. Some great records took years to mix. Mixing is very time consuming.

6. Make sure you do a good job all the way down the line. Start with great players who play great instruments. Make sure mic setup is great. Use good cables.

7. Fix all problems as you find them. Don't wait until later, because you might not ever get to it.

8. Avoid relying too much on "repair" plug-ins to correct mistakes, such as poor pitch or bad volume levels. Whenever possible, correct the performance at its source.

9. Pick the right people for the job. Listen to great music, understand what makes it great, and then seek out collaborators who share some of that spark. My students struggle with this. There are so many great players at the school, but they often want to record their friends, for their production projects. Then, these recordings become part of their portfolios, after they graduate.

    You want even your early practice recordings to be top notch. So, be realistic about the people you're recording.

10. Learn to communicate when something is going wrong. Learn to analyze why something doesn't sound good, and learn how to guide a performer towards making it sound better. Understand the roles of every instrument, and how to guide players back towards fulfilling their essential functions, when they stray. This type of communication requires experience—both as a listener and as a communicator. Recognize that it is an invaluable skill that can save a recording session. Try to develop it.

PROJECT 11.1. DEVELOP YOUR REFERENCE LIBRARY

Find at lease five high-quality, commercially successful recordings to use as your reference recordings. They should be in different styles that you are likely to produce on your own. Choose a track on each, and recreate the sound as closely as you can, using your own system. Periodically add new recordings, in different styles, to this library, and recreate their sounds.

CONCLUSION

You can learn a lot about mixing from bringing engineers to your own home studio. Learn from them, and incorporate their suggestions into your next mix.

Each time you record and mix a project, you will get better. Your ears will become more attuned to the process, and you will eventually gain a style of your own. Record your tracks carefully. If your mix conveys the mood and intention of the music, sounds good, and suits the medium in which it will be played, you have done well.

CHAPTER 12

Sound Processing

ONCE YOUR BASIC VOLUME LEVELS AND PANNING ARE SET, sound processing allows you to create or adjust overall ambience, dynamic level, stereo field, and many other parameters by using reverbs, delays, compressors, limiters, expanders, companders, noise gates, external EQs, multi-effect units, pitch changers, and other equipment. You apply these effects to your recorded tracks to create a recording that is unified, creative, and conveys the message of the music to the listener. This chapter is a reference, describing many different types of these effects.

Using Effects

It is common for beginning engineer/producers to overuse sound-processing technology. Why? Because they can! So before delving into *any* detail on this equipment, remember this: use discretion and taste. As the writer, you should know what you want the final product to sound like. That is your engineering goal. Each time you add a sound-processing device into the signal path, you alter the sound and the mix.

As you read this, technology is evolving. Many sound-processing effects that used to be individual pieces of hardware are now provided in sequencing and editing programs as plug-ins. Regardless of whether the effects come from outboard equipment or internal software plug-ins, they all work on the same principle; the format doesn't change the purpose or application.

Sound processing enhances the aural landscape of the music. It is helpful to know in advance the sound-processing techniques you will need to use, such as reverb or echo/delay to simulate a particular physical space and to define the nature of the piece of music. For example, in a film score with a science fiction image of travel through the universe, the enormity of the scene would not usually lend itself to a "dry" (no reverb or any ambience) and tight (very intimate) sound. The ambience of the music should fit the nature and feeling of the picture; open, flowing musical passages with somewhat long reverb would help to musically paint the picture. Conversely, a fast-moving action scene with up-tempo music and many "hits" (musical accents that enhance moments of action in the picture) would generally require a shorter reverb to maintain the tightness of the music and the music's integrity.

SOUND-PROCESSING EQUIPMENT: HARDWARE AND SOFTWARE

The sound-processing equipment in large studios is usually **hardware based,** meaning each piece of equipment is an individual device. The units are most often mounted into racks and connected to the console patch bay with cables hidden under the floor. Hence, the term **outboard gear.** It is now common, however, to use software-based sound-processing effects, called plug-ins. Sound-processing equipment and plug-ins can be divided into five categories:

1. **Ambient effects** are devices that alter or recreate the aural landscape in which the music is being heard. These include reverbs (digital, plate, spring, chamber), delays, and echoes.
2. **Dynamic effects** are used to control the volume of an audio signal. The most commonly used are compressors, limiters, noise gates, expanders, and de-essers.
3. **Equalization (EQ)** is used to alter the frequency content of the signal. Equalization is most often used in tracking and mixing to correct for sound anomalies and also place sounds in distinct positions in the aural landscape.
4. **Psychoacoustic effects** such as Aphex Aural Exciters and BBE Sonic Maximizers can help to restore lost overtones and high-end "breath" to tracks in which these parameters have been lost.
5. **Pitch-based effects** include harmonizers, auto tuners, and transposition devices used to add many special effects and to correct intonation problems.

The trick is in knowing how to utilize effects in a musical and purposeful manner. The final mix can be ruined by overusing, underusing, or not using effects. Using effects requires musicality and ingenuity, just as composing does.

AMBIENT EFFECTS

REVERB AND ECHO

An echo is a single discrete reflection of a sound wave. When there is an infinite amount of echoes or reflections off of many surfaces within a contained area, reverberation occurs. Reverb is most often used as the primary source of ambience in modern-day recording.

A reverb unit should be the first effects processor that you get. A versatile and powerful digital reverb unit can be a very expensive item, but there are plenty of very good affordable reverb units that can meet most needs. Furthermore, the plug-in packages (small programs that run within a larger program), when combined with digital audio programs, can be of a very high quality.

We experience reverberation all of the time, but are usually not consciously aware of it unless it is extreme, such as in a large church or gymnasium. If you have ever experienced sound in an anechoic chamber (a room with no sound reflections), you understand how much reverb is part of our everyday ambience. Compare the sound of speaking to a friend in a small room with a carpeted floor, curtains, and soft furniture, to conversing in a large empty gymnasium.

Throughout musical history, ambience has been an integral part of the mood that compositions create. For example, Baroque composers such as Bach, Handel, Vivaldi, and Monteverdi were well aware that their music would most often be performed in a large church and wrote their music accordingly. The best way to appreciate the authentic mood of Bach's choral music is to listen to it in a hall with much reverberation. Likewise, Bach's organ pieces were conceived for a large church organ and sound best with the reverberation that a cathedral provides. The music just wouldn't sound right in a nightclub played on a Hammond B3. Conversely, jazz, rock 'n' roll, or similar contemporary music isn't as effective in a church because the mood and intimacy is more suited for a club or concert arena.

Each room has its own acoustical characteristics, depending on its shape and size, construction materials, number of windows, and type of sound insulation. A large room or concert hall is going to create a lot more reverberation than the stage of a small club with a low ceiling. In the early days of recording orchestras, the intent was to replicate the sound of the performance, including the sound of the room or hall in which the orchestra performed. Microphones were set up in order to pick up the entire sound and capture the natural ambience.

To really understand how to make the music sound natural and well mixed, you must envision the ambience under the preferred circumstances. I once engineered a concert in a large church with organ, choir, cello, flutes, and recorders. The sound of the church was wonderful and the final mixes needed no additional reverb, because the microphones captured the sound of the church sanctuary. The ambience of the church created a natural and holistic recording of the concert with all of the emotional intimacy the audience experienced. If you were recording the same instruments in a studio and wanted to recreate the effect of a church space, you would need to add a reverb that could emulate that ambience.

Remember: reverb is an *added* sound that has to be mixed with the dry, unprocessed sound. Just as the reverberation in a concert hall is *not* the actual sound of the instruments but an entity unto itself, so is the ambience created in the studio. This is why you will usually return the reverb to another track or dial on the console and *blend* it with the original dry tracks.

There are several kinds of reverb, including: chamber, spring, plate, and digital. Each has unique sound characteristics.

Chamber Reverb

Shown in figure 12.1, chamber reverb (sometimes referred to as an echo chamber) was one of the earliest forms of reverb in recorded music. Though prevalent during the 1950s and 1960s, pure chamber reverb is rarely used today and exists in very few studios.

Chamber reverb is created in an empty room that is usually adjacent to the recording studio control room. The room's surface is commonly made of ceramic tiles or some other very reflective material. A speaker is placed at one end of the chamber and a microphone at the other end. The engineer sends the audio signal(s) to the speaker, and the room's surfaces reflect the sound. The microphone picks up this reverberation and returns the signal to the console, where it is mixed in with the dry sound.

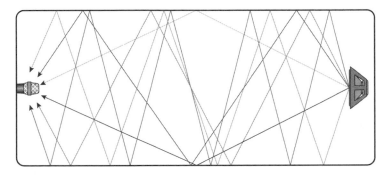

Fig. 12.1. Chamber Reverb

Spring Reverb

Although few recording studios, if any, use spring reverb as their main reverb unit, you are probably familiar with the sound. The Fender Twin Reverb amplifier has a built-in spring reverb that gives the amp its characteristic sound, one which is reminiscent of rock 'n' roll in the 1950s. You'll hear it in the playing of Les Paul, Chuck Berry, and Bill Haley.

Spring reverb requires a transducer (small metal plate that converts sound waves into a tiny electrical current) and a speaker. The transducer is attached to a spring or several springs suspended at both ends inside an enclosure. Audio signal is fed to the transducer, and reverb is created within the "spring tank" (the enclosure in which the spring is contained) and sent back to the console via another transducer(s) or speaker. The reverb track is then blended with the dry tracks.

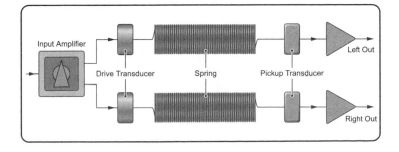

Fig. 12.2. Spring Reverb

Plate Reverb

Plate reverbs first appeared in the mid 1960s. Although rarely used today, they can still be found in larger high-end recording studios. The design of these reverbs was based on the same principle of sound wave reflection as chamber reverbs, but within an actual enclosed space containing a metal plate instead of a reflective chamber.

The plate reverb consists of a thin metal plate suspended in a soundproofed enclosure. A transducer similar to the motor of a moving-coil loudspeaker drive unit is mounted on the plate to cause it to vibrate. Two (for stereo) microphone-like transducers detect multiple reflections from the edges of the plates. A damping pad that can be pressed against the plate, thus absorbing its energy more quickly, varies reverb time. The plate would typically be mounted outside of the control room, with a remote control for reverberation time. The sound quality of a good plate reverb, such as the EMT plate, is very smooth and dense.

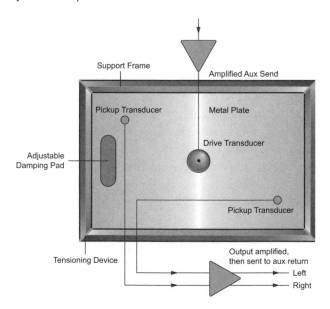

Fig. 12.3. Plate Reverb

Plate reverb has many limitations, such as lack of control in coloration, reverb time, and equalization.

Digital Reverb

By the early 1980s, digital reverb replaced plate reverb as the primary source of artificial reverb and is used almost exclusively today. Digital reverb creates tiny digital recordings of each reverberation, and these samples are stored on memory chips. Using mathematical algorithms to duplicate the randomness of actual reverberations, these units authentically duplicate a multitude of ambient spaces.

One of the earliest pitfalls of digital reverb was that, unlike plate or chamber reverb, it did not act on the principles of natural acoustics. Frequency and early reflection (the very first reflections of sound from near the sound source) determined how realistic reverb sounded. The lack of digital memory for sample storage limited the number of reverb algorithms that could be contained, so you could only choose between a small number of parameters, usually reverb length and room size.

Companies that pioneered digital reverb, such as Lexicon, eventually addressed this problem by allowing the engineer to select a variety of parameters within the unit itself. Now, digital reverb plug-ins allow the choice of specific reverbs from a menu of sounds, such as "concert hall," "small room," "large room," and "auditorium." The room size and type of reverb (spring, plate, or chamber) can be set. It is not uncommon to have controls on the front panel to adjust parameters such as frequency selection, cutoff filters, pre-delay, and early reflection to emulate an acoustic reverb. Even better, many units allow the user to save settings.

Control Parameters on the Typical Reverb Unit

Figure 12.4 illustrates the front face of a generic digital reverb unit. The sliders simulate the top-end Lexicon units, but most often, you use the digital interface on a plug-in, or select from an LCD menu. The diagram shows some of the basic parameters found on most reverbs, though the Lexicon 224 and 480L, which are common in most high-end recording studios, have far more variables.

Fig. 12.4. Generic Reverb Unit

Input/Output, with Matching LED. These dials control the input of the dry signal and the output of the effected signal. The LED gives the engineer an indication if the input signal is clipping (distorting). *As with all effects, if the signal is distorted coming in, it will be distorted going out.* Always ensure that all audio signals are not distorted.

Time. All modern digital reverbs have a setting for reverb time. The illustration shows time parameters variable from 0.1 seconds to 480 seconds. This setting controls the length of the reverb tail, or time on reverb onset until it disappears. This is probably the most important of the initial parameters and is crucial in making your recordings sound natural. Very short and very long reverbs can sound extremely disturbing. It is interesting to note that reverb time is considered the period of time that the reverberation is above –60 dB. Below this point the reverberation is considered inaudible.

Size. This slider controls room size and works in conjunction with reverb time. This control allows you to vary the size of the apparent space and is usually designated in meters. I mentioned previously that in early recordings, before separate reverb units, the engineer would consider the room ambience and place microphones accordingly. The size of the room determines many characteristics of the reverb, but primarily a feeling of space. Always consider the live space you are trying to simulate and select room size accordingly.

Pre-delay. Pre-delay is the time between the original sound source and the onset of the reverberation. Usually measured in milliseconds (thousandths of a second), this is a very important parameter in determining the ambience of the space and the way the listener will subconsciously perceive the effect. A long pre-delay will indicate a large room, whereas a very short pre-delay will imply a small room.

Feedback. This slider controls the feedback of the pre-delay on a graduating scale from –99 to 99. In simple terms, the feedback setting determines the number of times an echoed signal is repeated or fed back into the delay to be repeated again. A good analogy would be the first echo in a canyon, after your initial "hello." Chances are good that you will continue to hear your voice repeating as the first echo bounces off the wall of the canyon once again and returns to you, albeit much more quietly.

Diffusion. The diffusion setting is another way of controlling reverb density and helps to define the clarity and transparency of the reverb. Just as light can be diffused, so can sound. The number and type of reflective surfaces determine how freely the reverberation will move around. The more reflective surfaces there are, the more diffusion you will have. The density of the reverb will be greater and the thickness will be apparent.

Mix. This is a balance control between the dry sound and the reverberation added to the sound. This control is applied primarily when a reverb is used as an insert in the signal path. That is, instead of the engineer sending the dry signal to the reverb and returning the reverb on another track, the dry signal is blended with the reverb inside of the reverb unit. The only occasion for which you might use the reverb as an insert would be if you had used all of your auxiliary sends and were using a particular reverb for only one particular sound, such as the lead vocal or snare drum.

REVERB TIPS

- Use reverb musically. The reverbs, particularly short reverbs, can help the imaging at mix, but too many can confuse the clarity of the sound and distort the overall ambience of the project. Assign the main reverb (this is assuming there are several reverbs at your disposal) to the "overall" ambience. Use subsequent reverbs to accentuate particular instruments such as toms, background percussion effects, and so on.
- When mixing, always check the reverb returns to make sure that they are centered in the audio image. A mix can be confusing if the reverb is off center.
- Be judicious in using reverb on low-pitched instruments such as bass, bass drum, and bass synth. Reverb on low instruments can fill up the mix and create a muddy sound.
- Avoid using long reverbs on the main focal point of your mix. A long reverb will make a voice or instrument sound distant and therefore harder to bring out in the mix. Sometimes a little pre-delay on the focal point of your mix can aid in the clarity of the overall imaging.
- When possible, while recording synthesizers, track them dry without their own built-in reverb, and use your outboard reverbs at mix time to have better control of the overall imaging. This helps to create a more homogeneous sound.
- At some point in your mix, solo the reverb(s) to see how they are sounding. Sometimes a muddy mix can be the result of a stray low-end "bump" in the EQ of the reverb, or a low instrument being fed to the reverb unintentionally. You have to check that the clarity of the reverb is equal to the clarity of the other tracks.

The reverb unit is one piece of equipment about which you should learn as much as possible. Experiment with different settings and what they do to sound. Try the extremes to get a feel for each parameter. It may seem like some of the features contained within a reverb are more than you would ever need, but there may be a time when you will find these features can add that extra quality to the mix.

My engineering improved dramatically when I realized that the reverb was *another* sound in the music. Treating it with the care and sensitivity you give to the recorded tracks will help to enhance the final product.

DIGITAL DELAY (ECHO)

Digital delay (DDL), shown in figure 12.5, provides the foundation for many effects, including doubling, flanging, and chorusing. When the audio signal enters the unit, a digital sample (digital recording) of the sound is created, and is played back with a delay in time selected by the user.

Delay is generally measured in milliseconds (ms), or thousandths of a second. Any delay over 30 ms is very apparent, so use this setting with caution. When using delay settings of over 100 ms, pay particular attention to the tempo of the song. The delay should closely match the tempo of the piece, or you will most likely affect the groove (of course, you may be trying to achieve that effect).

The selection of available delay times on most DDL units is quite broad, from 1 ms to 10+ seconds. The feedback control on the delay allows the user to repeat the signal an infinite amount of times. This is done by looping the sampled signal within the unit. The single repeat of a signal is usually less desirable, but can work quite well in certain instruments or parts in a piece that has a fast tempo. Be judicious when using longer delay times because they take up a lot of sonic space in the mix. There are times when a delay can be used out of tempo to give the impression of a random "disappearance" of a particular sound, but this use is unusual.

Slapback

Another form of delay without modulation is **slapback**. Slapback is a very rapid return of an audio signal—in other words, a quick echo or any delay above 50 ms to about 100 ms. This can be used for a special effect in your mixes, particularly in emulating the sound of older recordings. Norman Petty's early recordings of Buddy Holly clearly demonstrate slapback. (They used tape delay in those days.)

Slapback can be used on a snare drum to create the feeling of a performance in a very small room, as well as to simulate a flam (a very quick two-stick hit on the snare) effect. Slapback works well on bass drum in the pop idiom. It simulates a club or arena reflection of the low frequency without the muddiness of reverb. A very short delay time can also bring out slap bass in a mix.

A doubling effect can be achieved by using delay from 25 ms to 50 ms. This is commonly used to give tracks depth and presence. The dry signal is sent to the delay and returned to another track, but delayed by the amount selected. This simulates the doubling effect. (However, even the finest delay does not duplicate the effect of natural doubling and can sound very artificial at times. If you have the time, it is better to get two excellent performances and combine them. You will be surprised at how it fills up the mix without being overbearingly loud.)

Delay between 1 and 30 ms can thicken a sound. This works effectively on bass, bass drum, and most other instruments in which you want a fuller sound, but don't want to use reverb.

Unlike reverberation, delay creates a simulated echo. The repeats are consistent in length and size, eliminating the random nature of reverb. Also, the equalization differences found in reverberation are often eliminated from the true delay. To create a spacious ambience, quite often a delay will be mixed in with the dry signal. A long delay time with moderate feedback will allow a relaxed, floating, elegant feel. Pat Metheny's guitar is a great example of delay being used for this purpose.

An effective use of delay is to pan the returned delay opposite to that of the dry signal. By panning the delayed signal to the opposite side and keeping the volume a little quieter than the dry signal, you can create the impression that there is a quiet echo in the background. An album I recently mixed had a track of seven a cappella vocal parts, all improvising. I used delay in this way to thicken the sound and help bring out the individuality of each part. Figure 12.5 shows the controls on a generic delay unit.

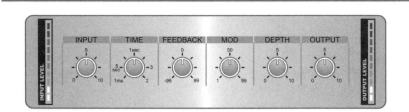

Fig. 12.5. Generic Delay Unit

INPUT controls the signal entering the delay. It has a matching LED indicator to show distortion at input.

TIME controls the delay time—the distance in time between the original signal and the repeated sample.

FEEDBACK controls the amount of echo repeats. It typically uses a graduating scale from –99 to 99. The negative numbers indicate an apparent reverse feedback (phase reverse), while the positive numbers allow for the increase in the amount of repeats of the sampled signal.

MOD is the Modulation parameter control. The gradation from 1–99 allows the increase of the variation in pitch from small to large. At its fullest setting, modulation can create a huge "whirling" sensation (also known as "flanging").

DEPTH controls the amount of apparent modulation in combination with the original delay. The wider the depth, the more modulation is used in the output.

OUTPUT controls the overall output and has a matching LED. The output control is very important on delay units, since overuse of internal feedback will create a loop than can distort the output signal.

Doubling, Chorusing, and Flanging

The use of the digital delay changes dramatically when the modulation and depth parameters are incorporated. Modulation changes the pitch of the entire delay signal, including the space between the repeats. Depth controls the amount of modulation that is incorporated into the delayed signal, resulting in a more powerful modulated effect. It is with these parameters that the effects of doubling, chorusing, and flanging are created.

Doubling is created when a short delay time is modulated slightly. In order to simulate a doubling effect with vocal or instrumental track(s), you have to understand how this would sound if actually performed by two people. Even though two voices or instruments play in unison and are *apparently* playing the identical note, there are actually tiny differences in pitch and timing between them. (This phenomenon makes a string section of an orchestra or a vocal chorus sound full and rich. If each musician played identically, they would just sound like one instrument or voice amplified.)

In order to duplicate a doubling effect electronically, the pitch of the original signal needs to be modulated (altered) ever so slightly. The modulated signal is combined with the original signal (at the original pitch.) Use a very short delay time of 16 to 30 ms with no feedback and a gentle modulation setting. The depth setting should also be subtle. Because the delay is now creating a pitch "revolving" around the original signal, it sounds like two people singing at the same time. Using the panning for imaging and reverb for unifying the sound can be a very effective method of thickening up a single isolated track. This is also a very effective way to "fatten" up a sound, make it wider in the stereo field, mask small intonation problems, and create interesting special effects.

Chorusing uses the same principles as doubling, except that chorusing refers to the effect stemming from a group of people singing (a chorus) or playing at the same time (rather than having one person singing the same track twice). This is also accomplished by the use of a relatively short delay time but with a wider modulation, and wider depth. Chorusing creates a fuller sound, which fills up space in the overall image. This effect is particularly useful for widening thin-sounding mono tracks of keyboards and guitars. Chorusing works very well with **synth pads** (sustained chords played by a synthesizer, usually a string- or voice-type sound), making them sound smoother and more present in the mix without being louder. Just like doubling, chorusing can be used to disguise small intonation errors.

Flanging is a short delay with extreme modulation and depth settings. The feedback can vary, but usually remains on the quick side. Flanging creates a somewhat heavy, swirling effect around the original sound and might be described as an "underwater effect." This is often used on vocals in pop music to give them a mid-rangy, slightly psychedelic effect.

Stereo delays are ordinarily found in multi-effects units, but are also contained in many dedicated stereo delay units. A delay that has a stereo output can create very interesting effects. A simple left/right delay with delay times of 100 ms in the left channel and 130 ms in the right channel can widen a thin mono signal. These units can pan the delay back and forth, contain variable modulation to generate a swirling effect, create stereo flanging, and create other effects.

DYNAMIC EFFECTS

COMPRESSORS AND LIMITERS

A compressor is a sound-processing device that, in its simplest terms, narrows the dynamic range (distance from quietest moment to loudest moment). The compression of the signal starts at the **threshold**—the setting at which processing takes place. The amount of compression that occurs on signals above the threshold is measured as the ratio between the uneffected signal and the compressed signal.

Limiting is used most often to compensate for the constant changes in louder volumes of the program material. The engineer sets the limiter to detect peaks in the material and instantaneously reduce the gain level, therefore preventing distortion. Just as instantaneously, once that peak has passed, the audio signal reverts to its actual level. Limiting sets a safe range of level within the program. When the volume of the program material is in the safe range, the limiter has no effect. The ratio of a limiter is very high, usually greater than 8:1. That is, 8 decibels of dry signal above the threshold will be reduced to 1 decibel.

Compressors and limiters are used so that:

- a particular instrument or vocal remains present throughout a piece of music
- a loud passage will not distort
- the final mix has a punchier, more unified sound
- the dynamic range of a track will be restricted to a signal that a broadcast transmitter can carry comfortably

Compressors are used frequently in broadcast media, such as television and radio. Broadcast media are required to meet government standards in the transmission of audio signals. The larger the dynamic range, the more power required to carry that signal. Transmitters would have to be extraordinarily powerful to carry an audio signal with a full and extreme dynamic range. Hence, jingles, television soundtracks, narration—and all program material, for that matter—are compressed either at the recording studio or at the broadcast station. At times, program material is compressed in both situations.

Perhaps more than any other effects, the use of compression and limiting is truly an art form. No matter how fine the quality of the compressor, there is always going to be some signal degradation. You have to hone your ears, weighing the positive effects versus the change in sound quality.

Humans have the ability to hear a wide dynamic range—from the quietest sounds in the forest to the loudest sounds, such as jack-hammers and jumbo jets. However, when reproducing this dynamic range electronically, there are dynamic-range restrictions, which compressors and limiters help in addressing.

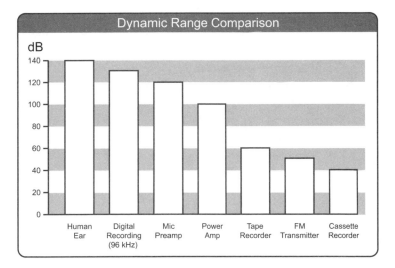

Fig. 12.6. Dynamic Range Comparison

Good, strong recorded sound lies between noise (unwanted recorded signal) and distortion (garbled recorded signal). The **noise floor** represents the inherent noise produced by a particular piece of equipment, such as tape hiss, transistor noise, electronic hiss, or a 60-cycle electronic "hum." If the audio signal is very low, it gets masked by the noise floor. This occurs when recording at a low level. When played back, there is a lot of noise and very little music. Figure 12.7 illustrates the limited useful operating region of recording to tape.

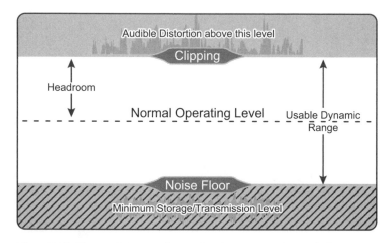

Fig. 12.7. The useful operating region between noise and distortion

Other items that enter the noise floor could include a signal that is too low in a reverb, too little level on analog tape, or audio signal that is too soft for a power amp to reproduce quietly. Interestingly enough, our ears tend to allow for the noise, somehow ignoring it when the audio signal is louder than the noise. This is known as "masking."

On the other hand, when the program material is too loud, *distortion* is created, either in the form of amplifier overload, extreme tape saturation, or digital clipping. The area between normal operating level and distortion or clipping is referred to as *headroom*. Within the normal operating level, transient peaks, or the initial attack of sound must be handled. The compressor instantaneously reduces the signal level to prevent this momentary "peak" from distorting and to keep it in the headroom area.

Digital recording eliminates the problems associated with tape hiss. However, the compressor is just as important in the digital world as in the analog world, because digital recording still functions on the principles of normal operating level and headroom. Just as with analog tape, the digital signal can be overloaded and become distorted.

Recording vocalists can pose particular dynamic range issues that compression can help remedy. Vocalists often have a large dynamic range. Recording the signal too low in order to compensate for the loud areas of the performance will result in a signal that will be barely audible when the singer sings quietly. Conversely, if you compensate for quiet sections by bringing the level up, you run the risk of surpassing the headroom and distorting the signal when it gets loud. Hence, the compressor becomes a very useful tool in controlling the dynamic range during vocal tracking sessions. The compressor is also very useful on instruments such as bass guitar, guitar, and drums, which have a tendency to create large transients (bursts of sound).

Figure 12.8 illustrates the layout of a simple generic compressor/ limiter, showing the basic functions found on most brands. These include Output Volume, Bypass Switch, LEDs to indicate input and gain reduction, Attack, Release, Threshold, and Ratio.

Fig. 12.8. Generic Compressor

INPUT LED indicates the level of audio signal entering the unit.

GAIN reduction LED indicates the amount of reduction in level when the compressor is functioning.

ON/OFF switch switches the unit on and off.

BYPASS switch, when depressed, bypasses the compression circuitry. This is generally used to compare the uneffected signal with the effected signal.

THRESHOLD sets the level at which the input signal will start to be compressed. For example, when the threshold is set to –10 dB, any audio signal above –10 dB will be compressed/limited.

RATIO sets the ratio of compression to audio signal. The setting of 1:1 represents unity gain, or no compression. A setting of 2:1 would be a very gentle compression and would reduce 2 decibels of input signal *above the threshold* point to 1 dB. 10:1 would be a very strong compression, reducing 10 dB of input signal above the threshold to 1 dB. Strong compression is generally used for limiting areas that are very dynamic.

ATTACK allows the user to set the amount of time between the first input of the signal and the time that the compressor actually starts to operate. For example, when set to 100 ms, the compressor will wait for the period of 100 ms after the initial signal goes above the threshold to use the compression circuitry. This way, the user can set the compressor to ignore transients that would be undesirable to compress.

RELEASE allows the user to set the release time of the compressor. When set to one second, the compressor will sustain the compression for a period of one second after the initial transient. This is very powerful control for using the compressor as a sustain device.

OUTPUT controls the overall output level of the unit after compression.

Remember: When recording, ensure that optimum signal is recorded, whether analog or digital. Otherwise, if your recorded signal is too low, your faders will be disproportionate during mixing. When you bring a poorly recorded track up in level to balance with the remaining tracks, noise will also increase accordingly.

The compressor/limiter is necessary in any studio as a fundamental signal-processing unit. When investing in your own studio, buy the best device you can afford. The compressor affects the overall frequency response and clarity of the sound, thus an inexpensive compressor on the voice can make it sound thin and, often, intolerable. In contrast, a good tube compressor is a very warm and smooth-sounding device. If set properly, it can be utilized with minimum degradation of sound quality. In the digital domain, there are also many good compressor plug-ins available.

DE-ESSERS

The de-esser is one of the most appropriate names given to any device in the recording field. It's a limiter or compressor dedicated to the elimination of those specific frequencies caused by sibilant "s" sounds from vocalists and voiceover artists. The de-esser can be set to take effect anywhere from 3 kHz to 10 kHz. Most of the sibilant sounds from the male voice occur at the low end and on the female voice, in the high end. Use EQ to isolate the frequency at which the sibilance is most pronounced and apply limiting or compression to that area to minimize the sibilance.

Take great care in the use of de-essing. Too much de-essing, or any compression or limiting for that matter, can make a track sound muffled. Too little will not correct the problem, but will result in some signal degradation.

EXPANDERS

The expander is a gain-reduction device that is generally used to reduce noise. Its function is essentially the opposite that of a compressor; effect takes place after the input level falls *below* a certain threshold. The effect is called expansion because of its relationship to the audio before the threshold is reached. The apparent result is to make the audio before the gain reduction sound louder by reducing the volume of the lower end of the audio. Expanders are used to prevent instrument and tape noise when the audio falls below an audible threshold.

DUCKERS

The ducker is another type of gain-reduction device. This device is keyed, or triggered, by an external audio source. It is often used in the broadcast medium when a DJ speaks over an audio track (usually music). When the DJ's voice reaches the preset threshold, the gain-reduction circuitry ducks, or lessens, the level of the audio track by a set ratio. That way the DJ doesn't have to scream over the top of the audio track or adjust its volume manually.

NOISE GATES

The noise gate serves as an "electronic gate" that opens to allow desired audio signal through, and helps to eliminate unwanted electronic noise. Noise gates open when signal achieves a preset volume (threshold) and close when the signal falls below that threshold. If music is recorded properly, noise will be adequately masked while the program material is playing. However, sometimes when the audio signal is very soft or silent, amplifier noise, tape hiss, reverb noise, and other noise may still be present. The noise gate is an electronic means of automatically "pulling the fader down" or muting a track.

There are dedicated noise gates, noise gates that are combined with compressors, and noise gates that are integrated into multi-effects units. Most noise gates react within a matter of microseconds (millionths of a second) and can therefore open in time to preserve the initial transient of any signal source. Most gates contain controls to affect the envelope (shape) of the audio signal.

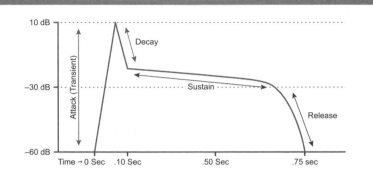

Fig. 12.9. This diagram represents a lateral view of a sound source, a snare drum hit.

ATTACK. The initial transient or attack of incoming audio.
DECAY. The first quick reduction in audio level from initial attack to sustained sound.
SUSTAIN. The length that the sound holds without noticeable gain reduction.
RELEASE. The moment that sound energy is released and becomes inaudible.

As an example, assume that the toms are gated, but are too loud and sustain too long when the gate is open. You can decrease the release time and output and, subsequently, the toms will be quieter and have less sustain than the actual sound source.

The engineer can use the gate to eliminate breaths between lines of a vocal, isolate certain microphones in order to eliminate unwanted leakage from other room microphones, remove buzz from the bass guitar when it is not being played, or exclude amp noise in quiet sections.

The noise gate can also be used to create new sounds. A popular technique is to use the key input, allowing one instrument to be gated by another. (When set to use a key input, the device will be triggered by another sound input.) For example, the bass guitar can be triggered by the bass drum. The bass guitar can be allowed through most of the time at a modest level, but it will come through at full level when the bass drum is played. This gives the impression of a stronger bass guitar attack whenever the bass drum is played, creating a tighter sound.

Figure 12.10 is an illustration of a typical noise-gate control.

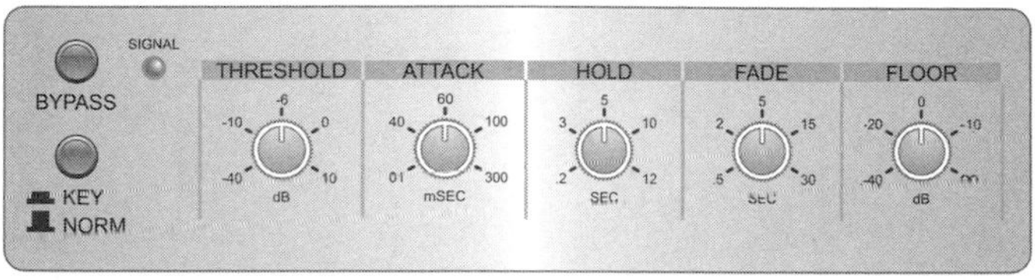

Fig. 12.10. Generic noise gate

BYPASS. This button bypasses the noise-gate circuitry. This enables the engineer to do a comparison between the effected sound and uneffected sound, or check that no desired audio signals are being gated.

KEY/NORMAL Switch. This button selects the input mode. When Normal is selected, the circuitry of the gate is connected to the audio signal being gated. When the Key button is selected, the gate-detection circuitry will be triggered (keyed) by an external signal entering at the Key input at the back of the effect unit. When Key is selected, the external signal will gate the signal that is connected to the normal audio input on the back panel.

THRESHOLD LED. This indicator will illuminate when the signal is above the threshold that is selected. This way the engineer can confirm that the gate is being triggered at the desired level.

THRESHOLD. This controls the level at which the gating circuitry will be triggered. The most effective way to set this control is to turn it up fully, then slowly ease it back until the undesirable signal is gated and you only hear the desired audio signal.

ATTACK. Attack controls the time in which the gating circuitry reacts to an incoming audio signal. Even though it might seem logical to have the attack set to respond as quickly as possible, occasionally an electronic pop occurs when a signal with a sharp transient quickly moves from silence to a high output level. Changing the attack time will eliminate this problem while maintaining the transient. This control is used for special effects and to "soften" the gating circuitry.

HOLD. The Hold control allows the gate to remain open even after the signal has fallen below the threshold level that would close the gate. During the Hold cycle, the gain of the gate is wide open. Only after the Hold time has elapsed does the gate fade out.

FADE. As soon as the Hold cycle has finished, the gate will close at a rate determined by the time set on the Fade control. On some noise gates, the fade can produce smooth fades of up to thirty seconds.

FLOOR. Sometimes, it is undesirable for a gate to "close" fully. For example, a gate closing on a guitar amplifier might create a disturbing contrast between the silence and the audio signal and result in an unnatural break in the sound. It might be desirable to have some slight amp noise in the background even when the gate is closed. The gate will always allow the level set on the floor control through the gating circuitry, but will not eliminate all of the audio completely.

USES OF NOISE GATES

- They eliminate unwanted noise on silent portions of a given track.
- They eliminate unwanted audio picked up and recorded by microphones (e.g., snare drum on tom track).
- When keyed (triggered) by another device such as EQ or reverb, they create special effects, such as gating a reverb.
- When keyed by another sound source (such as another instrument's track), they tighten up performances (EQ bass guitar in gate, keyed by bass drum).
- They create fades by using longer release-time settings.
- They tighten up an uneven performance using very quick release time (eliminates some extraneous notes or sounds).
- In live-sound reinforcement, they "close" open microphones onstage when they are not being used (e.g., BG vocal microphones).

The judicious use of dynamic or gain-control effects is fundamental to the creation of good-sounding music. These effects bring many benefits to the overall sound, not the least of which is tightening up low-frequency instruments and smoothing out erratic dynamics in a performance. However, overuse can negatively affect the sound of the recording. Use these devices as sparingly as possible, particularly compression.

EQUALIZATION (EQ)

As discussed in chapter 11, EQ is among the very most important sound-modification tools. Sound can be shaped in many ways, but perhaps no effect is more significant than equalization (EQ). EQ can make your recordings sound full or thin. EQ "equalizes" the frequency response that the ear perceives, in effect giving the perception that all frequencies are at an equal level (a "flat response").

EQ is an integral part of all consoles, amplifiers, and synths. Many studios have outboard EQs in their racks, in addition to their console EQs, and all good digital audio software programs contain excellent EQ plug-ins. A good feature of the plug-ins is their user-friendly graphic interface, which allows you to "draw" the shape of the desired EQ curve, or drag the threshold marker while visually relating to the input signal.

Outboard EQ gives the engineer or small studio owner the opportunity to add an expensive EQ as an insert into a modest console. With the use of tube EQs, graphic EQs, and high-end, solid-state EQs, excellent equalization can be attained without the large expense of a $500,000 console.

Humans hear in the range of about 20 Hz to 16 kHz, but do not hear all frequencies equally. Nor do we hear frequencies in the same proportion; different volumes accentuate and diminish certain frequencies. For this reason, it is important to always monitor your work at different levels, especially at mix time.

Each sound combines multiple frequencies, but emits a predominant frequency (or range of frequencies). A bass drum usually sounds in the 30 to 100 Hz range. Inadequately grounded electronic equipment creates a 60 Hz (or 60-cycle) hum. Musicians often tune to the note A, which sounds at 440 Hz. If you listen intently to a television when it is on, it emits a frequency of around 15 kHz. That is the very top end of hearing for most people.

The Fletcher-Munson Curve (figure 12.11) demonstrates how we correct sound through the use of equalization in order to achieve a relatively flat response. The lower the level of the music, the more we have to boost the low and high ends to hear a fairly even frequency response.

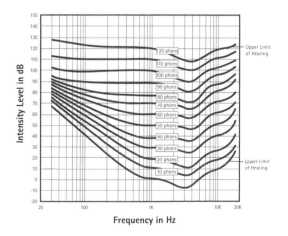

Fig. 12.11. Fletcher Munson

To fully understand EQ, it is essential that you learn how frequency and pitch relate to each other. A440 or 440 Hz is typically labeled as A4 on the keyboard. To find the frequency of one octave below a given pitch, divide by 2. Similarly, multiplying by 2 provides the frequency of the note one octave higher. For example, to find the frequency of A5, multiply A4 (A440) by 2 to arrive at 880 Hz; to find A3, divide by 2 and get 220 Hz. Figure 12.12 gives a complete version of the pitch-to-frequency relationships.

Pitch	Frequency	Pitch	Frequency	Pitch	Frequency
C9	8372	E6	1319	G3	196
B8	7902	D6	1175	F3	175
A8	7040	C6	1047	E3	165
G8	6272	B5	988	D3	147
F8	5588	A5	880	C3	131
E8	5274	G5	784	B2	123
D8	4699	F5	698	A2	110
C8	4186	E5	659	G2	98
B7	3951	D5	587	F2	87
A7	3520	C5	523	E2	82
G7	3136	B4	494	D2	73
F7	2794	A4	440	C2	65
E7	2637	G4	392	B1	62
D7	2349	F4	349	A1	55
C7	2093	E4	330	G1	49
B6	1976	D4	294	F1	44
A6	1760	C4	262	E1	41
G6	1568	B3	247	D1	37
F6	1397	A3	220	C1	33

Fig. 12.12. Pitch-to-Frequency Relationships

TYPES OF EQ

There are five main types of EQ: graphic, parametric, semipara-metric, shelving, and roll-off filters.

The **graphic equalizer** displays its settings on the front panel in a graph as a curve of particular frequency ranges that are either cut or boosted. It may contain anywhere from five to more than thirty bands; the most practical for studio use is the twelve- to fifteen-band version. The more bands, the more finely the EQ can be controlled.

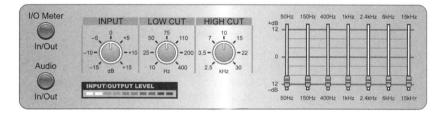

Fig. 12.13. Graphic Equalizer

The graphic equalizer (see figure 12.13) has numerous vertical sliders, or bands. Each band has a range of frequencies associated with it, giving the engineer great control over selecting particular frequencies. The problem with the graphic equalizer is that you cannot pinpoint any particular frequency, because you adjust a *range* of frequencies that is centered by the selected band frequency. For example, boosting 3000 Hz actually boosts a range of about 1500 Hz to 6000 Hz. The more bands on the graphic equalizer, the narrower each bandwidth that is affected by any adjustments and the more control you have.

One of the great advantages of using a graphic equalizer is that it allows you to make several EQ changes using a simple device. With most other EQs, each control can only make one adjustment. Also, the display of the equalizer is a great help in visually determining the frequency "shape" of the signal you are EQing.

Parametric EQ provides the greatest versatility and control of the frequency spectrum. Most high-end consoles offer at least two bands of parametric EQ in the mid range with frequency ranges that cross over into each other and into the high or low frequency ranges.

Figure 12.14 illustrates the layout of a typical parametric EQ. This one offers the engineer the choice of three different controls: frequency select, cut/boost, and Q (or bandwidth).

- The frequency-select control allows the engineer to center the EQ on a particular frequency.
- The cut/boost control is a volume control that adjusts how much of the effected frequency is added or subtracted from the original audio signal.
- The Q (bandwidth) control allows for the fine-tuning of the effected frequencies from a range of about one-third of an octave to three octaves on either side of the selected frequency.

The detailed control allows a variety of tasks, such as pinpointing and eliminating a ringing sound, a hum at a particular frequency, or excessive sibilance. It also enables the pinpointing of frequencies to boost in order to bring out the richness of a beautiful voice, cymbals, or low mids of a fretless bass. The fully parametric EQ is a wonderful effect if used musically.

Fig. 12.14. Parametric EQ

Semiparametric EQ is directly related to its counterpart, with the exception of the Q control. Like the graphic EQ, the bandwidth (Q) for each frequency is preset and not controllable by the engineer. There is still the option of cut/boost and frequency-selection switches. Although semiparametric EQ is not as versatile as its parametric counterpart, it is very effective and provides a great deal of control.

Shelving EQs contain preset frequency and bandwidth selection, and only a controllable cut/boost control, usually from –15 dB to +15 dB. Shelving EQs work like the treble and bass tone controls on a home stereo, but are labeled High and Low. Some mid-priced consoles contain shelving EQ on the high and low frequencies. Outboard devices occasionally include shelving EQ.

Roll-off filters, or bypass filters, generally provide only the control to turn the filter on or off. Very expensive consoles, like the SSL, allow the user to select a specific frequency to be filtered out, but most consoles have the frequency, level of cut, and bandwidth already preset. The two common roll-off filters are the high-pass (or low-cut) filter and the low-pass (high-cut) filter. Figure 12.15 illustrates how high-pass and low-pass filters work.

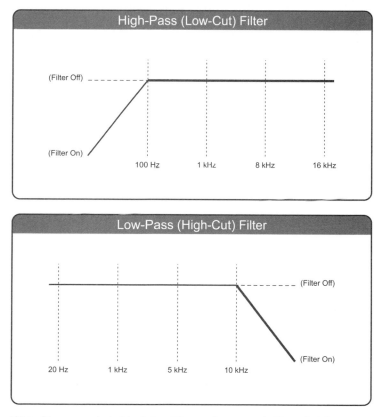

When filters are selected (on), the EQ curve is represented by a dark line.

Fig. 12.15. High-Pass and Low-Pass Filters

These filters are extremely useful. A high-pass filter, when engaged, allows high frequencies to pass through unaffected, while using filters to cut out very low frequencies. A low-pass filter acts in the opposite manner; it permits low frequencies to pass through unaffected, while cutting out very high frequencies. A high-pass filter can eliminate virtually all of the very low frequencies, such as a rumble, without affecting the integrity of the recorded track.

The low-pass filter is very good at getting rid of tape hiss on tracks that have low sounds and don't need the "air" of the high-frequency range, such as bass drum, acoustic bass, and electric bass.

PSYCHOACOUSTIC EFFECTS

Psychoacoustic effects alter the way sound is perceived in three dimensions: height, depth, and width. That is particularly intriguing, given the fact that people listen to audio in two dimensions (width and depth), yet still *perceive* height.

Manufacturers of audio equipment constantly develop new and exciting equipment to bring audio to life and expand the way in which sound is perceived. Audio equipment engineers and developers have created simple yet brilliant circuitry that gives the listener the implication of a wider stereo field, increased presence and clarity, and a broadened three-dimensional perception.

APHEX AURAL EXCITER

Every sound has a particular waveform. The primary pitch, even in spoken word, is termed the "fundamental." An infinite number of harmonics (overtones) exist above the fundamental, giving the sound character, breadth, and clarity. One of the most interesting devices available—the Aural Exciter manufactured by Aphex—was developed to help compensate for the electronic reproduction of music stealing the harmonics away from the original sound. It recreates those missing overtones without significantly increasing signal level.

This is a superior method of EQing certain sounds, because the Aural Exciter adds harmonics, thereby improving the sound's presence in the mix. Another benefit is that the increase in presence does not contain a similar boost in high-end noise that would be associated with increasing the high frequencies using EQ.

Aphex Aural Exciter contains an added feature called Big Bottom, which shapes the bottom end in the 20 Hz to 120 Hz range. It increases the presence of the low frequencies without actually boosting level or adding bottom through EQ.

BBE SONIC MAXIMIZER

As I was learning how to engineer and mix, quite often the results would sound dull. A salesperson recommended purchasing a BBE 802 and sending the lead voice or instrument—or the entire mix—through the device. I tried it, and the results were amazing. The BBE restored the breadth and clarity that had disappeared through the recording process.

BBE developed an effect that restores the brightness and definition of any signal passing through it. BBE addressed inherent problems in speaker design by recognizing that speakers' natural tendency is to add longer delay times to higher frequencies. The higher the frequency, the greater the impedance, or electronic resistance, that is created. Therefore, the listener receives the higher frequencies more slowly than the lower frequencies, resulting in an unnatural sound. The Sonic Maximizer corrects this by injecting a slight delay in the middle and lower frequencies, which allows high frequencies to be received first, and better replicates the way music is naturally heard. The Sonic Maximizer also augments the high and low frequencies in order to correct weaknesses of speakers to reproduce very low and very high frequencies, giving the appearance of a smoother, fuller frequency range in the audio.

PITCH-BASED EFFECTS

Digital technology has changed the face of external processing equipment. Nowhere is that more evident than in pitch and modulation effects. Devices such as simple pitch changers, octavers, harmonizers, and auto-tuners afford the engineer the ability to create unique combinations of effects and even fix weak tracks during the mix process. With digital pitch-based effects, the input signal is digitally sampled and then processed in the manner the user determines.

Eventide's multi-effects devices have led the way in this technology, especially in the areas of pitch-change capability and harmonization. The Eventide Model H3500 Ultra-Harmonizer is a contemporary top-of-the-line unit, featuring such capabilities as pitch shift, reverb, chorus, auto panning, delay, filter sweeping, time compression/expansion, 3D spatial imaging, and vocoder effects.

Pitch change has been around for a long time in the analog domain. Audio pioneers learned that varying the speed of a tape machine changed pitch, but had to solve a resulting problem: it also changed tempo. In the early days, pitch changers made the character of the original sound almost unrecognizable when modulated (pitch-changed). Thankfully, that problem has been solved. A sound can now be modulated by a pitch-change device and maintain the tempo and sound quality of the original.

An offshoot of the pitch changer is the harmonizer, which allows the user to add a harmony part to the input signal based on the capability of the device. The Eventide can harmonize in constant structure, meaning that you can assign an interval or chord structure and the unit will harmonize each input note in the same way. For example, if the harmony selected is major chords, and each input note is to be the tonic of the chord, the result will be a series of major chords built on every input pitch.

Perhaps even more amazing is the capability to harmonize diatonically to a given key, or even a scale. This feature can bring some remarkable effects. It is a great way to create harmony vocal parts from a single line. If the piece was in C minor, you could harmonize each input note with chords built on the C minor scale.

Harmonizers also allow for great doubling effects. Instead of using a simple delay to create doubling, some new devices can randomly modulate the sound within a very small pitch area, as well as create random delay, resulting in a very realistic doubling effect. I love what the stereo doubler does to the sound of the fretless bass; it creates a full bottom end without increasing the apparent gain.

Another great feature of this machine is time compression. Imagine you have written and recorded a film cue to fit a 30.2-second scene, but the film editor has just cut the scene to 29.8 seconds. You simply input the audio into the device, select the new length you wish the piece to be, in this case 29.8 seconds, and it will compress the audio to that length without changing pitch.

You will have to practice using each of these sound-processing devices, understand what they can do, learn the sounds that they can create, and know how to use them effectively. You should also listen to many recordings to experience how engineers have used sound-processing effects in musical productions.

Don't be afraid to use the audio techniques of the great producers and engineers—but always remember that the music comes first, and the effects and other technology are there only to enhance the power and emotion of the music.

PROJECT 12.1. CREATE AN EFFECTS JOURNAL

What effects do you own? Create a journal listing and describing each effects unit in your arsenal. List any outboard gear and then any effects plug-ins within any of your software, or that you have purchased separately. Classify them in accordance with the five families discussed in this chapter: ambient, dynamic, EQ, psycho-acoustic, and pitch-based.

PROJECT 12.2. COMPARE EFFECTS

Choose an effect that you have multiple version of: perhaps reverb or EQ. Figure out a way to A/B the same original signal being processed, alternately, by the two different effects units. Do they sound different? Is one better than the other? Or easier to use? Do this with as many effects as you can. Keep careful notes of your preferences.

PROJECT 12.3. LEARNING EFFECTS

For at least EQ, compression, and reverb, make sure that you master *every* control on the units you will use most often. Understand what each parameter does at minimal, moderate, and extreme settings. Experiment with one track and with several tracks together.

CONCLUSION

Though effects may be commonly overused, their judicious application to your mix can make your music sound "professional." Focus on mastering the basics of your most important effects units, and then move on to learn other common ones. Take notes to keep track of them, and feel free to experiment, when appropriate.

CHAPTER 13

Selecting Equipment

IT IS VERY EASY TO BECOME CONVINCED by the latest catalogs from music stores and computer software warehouses that your recordings will suffer if you don't purchase the latest equipment. But realize: much of the world's greatest music was written before electricity. *Sgt. Pepper's Lonely Hearts Club Band* was recorded with a 4-track tape machine! The latest advances in technology will not make you a better writer/producer. You don't want to have to work two jobs to maintain a gear addiction. You'll be more successful if you devote those hours to your music career—writing and promoting yourself.

I highly recommend buying some new and some used equipment. Smart and informed shopping online can be a great way to go. The best sources for information on recording technology and equipment are online sites, particularly eBay, but magazines such as *Electronic Musician, Keyboard, Mix,* and *Tape Op* can provide invaluable advice.

Every item in your studio doesn't have to be top of the line, although there are some items that you should not compromise on. If you have a limited budget, consider purchasing used equipment. In order of importance, spend as much as you can afford on:

- a fast computer with enough RAM, and a large monitor
- great sequencing software and hardware with powerful digital audio capabilities
- an excellent multitimbral synth (either software or hardware based) with a keyboard to use as a master controller
- a great condenser microphone with shock-mount clip and solid microphone stand
- great monitor speakers
- high-quality cables
- one good direct (DI) box
- one good pair of studio headphones
- a great tube compressor

IS HARDWARE DEAD?

There is ongoing discussion about whether the traditional methods of recording are giving way to the virtual software-based recording systems. The proponents of digital recording have been talking about the death of analog recording since the 1990s.

Many users believe that analog recording has better sound quality than digital recording. Proponents of analog tout its warmth, punchiness, and unity of sound. However, the newest advances in digital recording—particularly multitrack software such as Pro Tools, Digital Performer, and Logic—make it harder for the analog world to maintain a high-level market presence. The analog multitracks in many large studios sit idle most of the time. Higher sampling and bit rates, and more affordable and powerful computers and software, make digital recording preferable for most projects.

However, the recording console manufacturers who sell high-end professional equipment are still doing well, as they marry both the analog and digital worlds. The sound of a high-quality console with high-quality outboard gear using a digital recording system is favorable, if you can afford it. Many successful hardware manufacturers of consoles and outboard gear have expanded their product line to include their own software-based products. The good news for all of us is that, with the exception of the very highest level of recording equipment, the prices of all analog hardware continue to fall.

For many of us, the aesthetic of a piece of hardware and the holistic feel of turning knobs and pushing real buttons counts for a lot. Hardware doesn't require the conversion of analog audio to digital and, hence, there is a purity to the sound, particularly in the areas of equalization and compression. For these reasons, many engineers and producers still view hardware as a valuable and necessary component. Hardware is definitely not dead. It will continue to play an important role in recording by evolving and blending the best of the virtual elements and hardware features.

Items like CD and DVD burners, consoles, mic preamps, software, and so on can be bought very reasonably if you shop around. Start by looking through catalogs and reading periodicals to get an idea of what is current and what the future holds. Then go for some of the equipment from the past. Even a year can make a huge difference in the price of equipment. Borrow equipment if you can, and get some used synths. They can be really inexpensive!

Things to Buy New	Things You Can Buy Used
computer	microphones
external hard drive	controller keyboard
monitor	synthesizer modules
software	sound-processing effects (reverbs, compressors)
cables	power amps
speakers	direct boxes
digital interface	

Let's look into some of the most important equipment: recording devices (a computer and music recording software), loudspeakers and amplifiers, headphones, and other studio must-have equipment.

RECORDING DEVICES: MULTITRACKING

The multitracking device is a key component of your studio. Multitracks are the main machines onto which all of the individual tracks are recorded for stereo mix down. Today's software allows you to record many tracks onto a hard drive, limited of course by the computer's power and storage capacity. There are many varieties of multitrack recording software.

DIGITAL MULTITRACK RECORDERS

Computer-based digital recording has been around for many years now, and is here to stay. The Digidesign Pro Tools setup is the mainstay of high-end digital audio. Sequencing programs such as Digital Performer, Logic, and Cubase incorporate a powerful MIDI component and have digital recording components that are powerful enough to be used as stand-alone digital recorders. Most professional recording studios use Pro Tools as their main sequencing program because of its flexibility and high-end hardware (digital/analog converters), while most writers prefer to use the hybrid sequencing/digital audio software because of the powerful MIDI component. With computer-based recording, the hard drive is the recording medium, hence the term "hard-disk recording." The faster your computer is and the more RAM you have, the greater the power of your digital audio.

Although I am not a proponent of getting the latest and greatest, you are best served to get the newest and most powerful computer system that you can afford in order to run the digital audio system smoothly and efficiently.

> Digital music files can use up a lot of space on your hard drive. In order to get an idea of the power and storage required, consider that a mono audio track recorded at the 44.1 kHz sampling rate at 16 bits requires about 5 MB of storage per minute. For example, a 5-minute song with 24 tracks of digital audio would require 600 MB.

ANALOG/DIGITAL CONVERTERS

One of the most critical pieces of equipment in a quality digital studio is the analog/digital converter (D/A), often called an "audio interface." These devices convert audio signals to digital for editing and storage on disk. Your A/D converter might be a PCI card that is plugged into the computer motherboard, an external piece of hardware connected by USB or FireWire, or a rack-mounted hardware unit. For the powerful capabilities that these devices possess, the cost is very small. Get the best quality possible. Any weakness in this end of the process will result in a very poor sound, with loss of high frequencies, disappearance of quiet passages, and an overall grainy and brittle quality.

2-TRACK MACHINES

The 2-track machines are stereo devices that are most often used for listening or mix down. These include direct CD recorders, DATs, record players for LPs, CD players, stereo digital hard-disk recorders, and 2-track analog machines.

With the exception of devoted playback-only devices such as some CD players and record players, all of the other machines are used primarily for recording. The 2-tracks can also be used for playback of previously recorded material, editing of previous mixes, or transfer to other platforms. These machines are an integral part of every studio and should be the best quality you can afford.

The most common 2-tracks are the DAT machine (digital audio tape recorder) and the stereo analog tape recorders. The DAT player offers the conveniences of the digital world, including low signal-to-noise ratio, inexpensive tape costs, and compatibility in the digital domain.

The newest format being used for stereo mixes is the hard-disk format centered around a computer-based software program such as Peak or Pro Tools. In fact, as long as you have a high-quality analog-to-digital converter, you can record a stereo track onto any digital audio program, and subsequently have almost limitless editing capabilities.

Within the digital domain, you have the option of using many different platforms. It is possible to mix to DAT through the use of a SPDIF cable (a stereo digital transfer cable that keeps audio in the digital domain), transfer to a digital audio program, do editing, and then return the edited version to DAT via the same SPDIF cable. In addition, there are CD burners that can "burn" your mixes directly to CD.

AMPLIFIERS AND LOUDSPEAKERS

You can have the most wonderful console, outboard gear, and recording equipment, but if you have poor amplification and just a pair of cheap speakers, you will never be able to experience high-caliber recordings and mixes.

AMPLIFIERS

Common studio setups have at least three power amps: one for the main speakers ("the big ones"), one for the near-field monitors, which are smaller speakers positioned close to the engineer, and at least one for the headphone mix. All of these amplifiers take their feed from the different stereo outputs of the console.

Headphone amps must possess adequate power. Head-phones typically have a lot of impedance, or electrical resistance. (Loudspeakers do not have a large imped-ance—usually 4 or 8 ohms.) If you are powering several sets of headphones and want a clean sound without overloading the amp, power must be available. It is frus-trating to have the performers ask for more level (volume) in their headphones, only to find that the console is maxed out at the auxiliary outputs and the power amp is full and distorting.

If possible, stay clear of home stereo power amps and receivers. Although they can work fine as a third or fourth amp for monitoring, the addition of tone controls and other controls degrade the signal. Further, the manufacturers have not designed the components in these systems to be the quality required for use in a professional studio. The difference can become very clear when comparing the specification sheets of home receivers and pro amplifiers.

The qualities to look for in a power amp include:

- power
- frequency response—ability to effectively reproduce all frequency ranges
- signal-to-noise ratio—the ratio of audio to noise created by electronics; the lower the better
- THD, Total Harmonic Distortion—ability to create a "clean" sound
- crosstalk—leakage of one channel's audio into the other
- connectivity
- versatility

Power output is measured primarily in watts RMS, or the maximum output of continuous undistorted signal. Occasionally on cheaper amps, you will see measurements in watts of peak output. This is very misleading, because it only represents the output for a brief moment when a transient (the loudest part of a sound wave) is present. The only figure you should be interested in is RMS. Most high-end companies do not publish an output in peak watts, this being reserved for very low and occasionally mid-priced home systems.

The Crown CE 1000 studio power amp, still in use today, has the following power measurements, which represent the professional studio standard:

CROWN CE 1000	
	Power Output
2-ohm Stereo (per channel)	560W
4-ohm Stereo (per channel)	450W
8-ohm Stereo (per channel)	275W
4-ohm Bridge—Mono	1,100W
8-ohm Bridge—Mono	900W

Power Output refers to maximum average output (RMS) at a frequency of 1 kHz with 0.5-percent THD (very low distortion). A test tone of 1 kHz is used to test amplification. Bridge-Mono means that two stereo outputs are connected internally to make a single mono output.

You're best served by purchasing an amplifier with a very high power output. The goal is not to play the music loudly, but rather to use as little of the available power as possible to achieve the same volume. This results in a cleaner sound with greater frequency response, as the amplifier circuitry is not being driven as hard to produce the desired volume.

LOUDSPEAKERS

Speaker technology is always changing, and it is very exciting to witness the new innovations. The latest significant change is the advent of powered speakers—systems with built-in, high-quality amplification. This has eliminated the need for expensive power amps, particularly in the near-field monitor area.

A standard moving-coil loudspeaker system is very reliable and is therefore the backbone of most recording studios. Another type of speaker that is becoming increasingly popular, particularly in home computer usage, is the flat-panel system. The flat-panel system has high-quality sound reproduction, but lacks the durability of dynamic speaker systems.

It is generally a good idea to have several sets of speakers in your home studio. If the room permits, utilize a large set that can play cleanly and loudly. These speakers will often exaggerate the bottom end of the frequency spectrum and are effective for mixing more rhythmic music. The only problem with these systems is that the frequency response at very low volumes can sometimes suffer, as they need a fair amount of power to function properly.

The near-field monitors have become the mainstay of the speaker setup. They are so named because they are usually placed within five feet of the engineer. If you can only accommodate one speaker setup, this is the one to have. Near-fields are generally very high-quality speakers. They usually have a very good frequency response at relatively low volumes. Also, as opposed to the large speaker systems, whose sounds are greatly affected by the acoustics of the control room, the near-fields tend to be less prone to the anomalies of the control-room environment. Interestingly enough, some near-field speakers in common use are not always top of the line. Many studios utilize mid-line speakers such as the Yamaha NS10 series (not in production any longer but still readily available), which lack a little on both the bottom and high frequencies, but give a fair representation of the home-speaker response. Engineers like this kind of system, because if the mix sounds good on these speakers, it will sound good on many systems.

In order to simulate speakers that are found in low-end television sets and car radios, purchase inexpensive speakers. Any set of inexpensive speakers will work for this purpose. Even computer speakers offer a reasonable alternative.

It is usually best to get speaker enclosures that are direct radiators, meaning they transmit the sound waves directly into the room. If the speaker is not sealed tightly in the rear of the cabinet, the sound will also radiate from the back and sides of the speakers. The sound will reflect off of the back and side walls of the control room and create a deceiving sound quality that is not representative of the true speaker sound.

Also consider a "crossover system" for your setup. A speaker crossover built into the speaker system is adjustable at the rear of the speakers in higher-end studio models. The crossover filter takes the entire audio signal and divides it into frequency groups. Each frequency range is then sent to a particular speaker in the enclosure, which is designed to reproduce that frequency range effectively. For example, in a two-way system, the crossover sends the higher frequencies to the tweeter (a speaker specifically designed for high-frequency projection) and the woofer (a speaker specifically designed for lower frequencies). Three-way systems have a mid-range frequency as well. Although the design is usually apparent in appearance alone, the near-field monitors that I use, Tannoy NFM-8s (twenty years old), have the tweeter and woofer built into one speaker system. Most speaker manufacturers still produce this format, which projects sound from just one area of the speaker, creating a more homogeneous effect. An open port allows the lower-end frequencies created within the cabinet to escape.

Another speaker setup worth considering, particularly for multimedia, is the surround-sound setup. This comes in different formats, most commonly 5.1, or five speakers intended to be heard from one reference point. The ideal 5.1 setup places you sitting in the center of four speakers, two in front and two in the rear. In addition, the system contains a subwoofer, a special speaker that transmits only the lowest audible frequencies, such as the richness and the rumble experienced in surround-sound movie theaters. This setup is not common in studios doing music for CDs, but is becoming increasingly common for television work, as well as software, industrial music, and computer audio. There are also setups with 6.1, 7.1, 10.1, and now 10.2, or ten speakers from two reference points. In order to accommodate any of these setups, you need special equipment, such as amplifiers, multiple speakers, and subwoofers. Most of the newest professional software-based recording studios have wonderful surround-sound setups in their software console modes.

There is a huge variety of speaker designs. Research to find the system that best suits your needs. Before deciding which speakers to buy, listen to a familiar CD recording over the system. If the speakers reproduce the recording's familiar quality, they are probably a good choice.

MICROPHONES

Without at least one good microphone and knowledge of its use, you will rarely be able to record live performers in a way that will convey your writing talent positively. Imagine spending endless hours painting the most vibrant, colorful, and passionate work of art, only to have the public view it through several layers of sheer drapery. That is what improper microphone selection and placement can do to your recordings.

Microphone choice is quite often a matter of taste. Most types and brands of microphones have a unique purpose. At a music engineering convention seminar, someone once asked the well-known producer/engineer Bob Clearmountain what microphone he would use if he only had one choice and expense were not a factor. He chose the Shure SM57, a dynamic microphone that costs around $100—and that is significant, coming from someone known for his production and engineering work with Bon Jovi, Bruce Springsteen, the Rolling Stones, Paul McCartney, the Who, and Tina Turner. This microphone would never work as the only one recording a symphony orchestra in a large hall or intimate female vocal tracks to a soul ballad, but Clearmountain tends to record music on the heavier side and feels that this microphone delivers an appropriate sound.

TYPES OF MICROPHONES

There are five primary types of microphones: condenser, ribbon, dynamic, crystal (piezo), and carbon. The first three are the types commonly used in higher-end productions. The other two are rarely used in the production of music and their unique characteristics limit their use.

In studios today, the condenser and dynamic microphones are the most common. The ribbon, which is an older style and not as common, is used to recreate specific sound qualities reminiscent of older recordings. Of course, any microphone can be used at most any time.

Condenser. The condenser microphone (or electrostatic microphone) works on the principle of varying degrees of electrical energy between a movable diaphragm and rigid back plate. This microphone requires a voltage supply to provide the electrical current to both the diaphragm and back plate. The power is usually generated directly from the console (using a phantom power supply) and transmitted through the microphone cable. Two of the most famous versions of the condenser microphones are the Neumann U87 and the AKG 414, both incredible-sounding microphones.

Ribbon. The ribbon microphone uses a thin piece of pleated metal that is suspended between two poles of a magnet. When sound pressure moves the ribbon, a tiny electromagnetic signal is produced and sent to a transformer. The newer ribbon microphones have sturdier ribbons, but the older versions were very fragile and fell out of favor with engineers because of their expensive maintenance costs and lack of reliability. These microphones, with their unique sound and excellent frequency response, are a great option for recording, although they are not very common in the home-studio environment.

Dynamic. In a dynamic microphone, a movable diaphragm is attached to a wound coil that is suspended between two poles of a magnet. When the sound energy moves the diaphragm, the coil is moved between the poles of the magnet and an electromagnetic signal is transmitted through a wire attached to both ends of the coil. It is then amplified at the console. These microphones do not require any power source and, unlike the ribbon microphone, are very sturdy. The most common makes of dynamics are the Shure SM57 and SM58 and the Sennheiser MD421 and MD441.

Crystal. A crystal microphone (piezo) uses two pieces of a crystal, generally quartz or rochelle salt, placed in an airtight compartment. The piezo electric effect states that any stress applied between two suitably cut pieces of crystal will produce the desired electromagnetic field or voltage output, which generates sound. These microphones are rarely used in a recording studio. They are reserved primarily for use in budget cassette recording.

Carbon. Carbon, by virtue of its physics, converts sound energy into electrical energy. These microphones were most common in telephones and for other voice-related purposes. Invented in the early twentieth century, they were also used for early recordings. With a total frequency range of 300 Hz to 3 kHz, they have no use in a recording studio, other than for effect.

Specialty. There are many specialty microphones in use today. For music production, the tube microphone is a throwback to the early days of condensers, when transformers and power supplies were powered by vacuum tubes. Tubes add warmth and fullness to microphones. Eighty years ago, the tube(s) was in a large box on the floor attached by a cable to the microphone. Now it is located within the housing of the microphone itself. These microphones are generally very expensive.

Another specialty microphone introduced in the 1970s is the PZM, or Pressure Zone Microphone, designed by Crown International. The PZM is a thick metal plate about 5 inches on each side with a dynamic capsule mounted on its face. The PZM eliminates any sound from its dead side and can be attached to a wall in the studio or to the inside of a piano lid. This way, it eliminates many reflections and room ambience. The response on PZMs tends to emphasize mid-range frequencies. PZMs work well in conjunction with other microphones, or if placed properly, can sound great alone.

MICROPHONE DIRECTIONAL RESPONSE

An important aspect of choosing a microphone is knowing its directional response or polar pattern. These patterns indicate the areas surrounding the microphone in which the frequency response and volume best capture the full sound spectrum. On many modern microphones, particularly the more expensive condensers, up to three polar patterns can be selected.

Most dynamic microphones are specific in the pattern they produce and, therefore, have a specific use. There are four main microphone patterns: hypercardioid with its sister, supercardioid (unidirectional), cardioid, figure-8 (bidirectional), and omnidirectional. On the multi-pattern condensers such as the AKG 414 or Neumann U87, you have a choice of omni, figure-8, and cardioid.

The term "on-axis" applies to a situation in which a sound source is completely within the polar pattern that encompasses the frequency and volume-sensitive area of the microphone. Conversely, if a singer is "off-axis" on a microphone, he or she is not singing within the area around the microphone that picks up the full nature and energy of the sound.

Cardioid. The cardioid microphone, so called because of the heart shape of its polar pattern, is common. It is found in both condenser and dynamic microphones. Figure 13.1 shows the polar pattern and gives a good representation of the sound pickup within an area of about 160° around the front of the microphone. These are very good all-purpose microphones and can be used in an isolated area quite effectively. The ambience and sound from the back of the microphone is eliminated to a great degree.

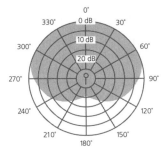

Fig. 13.1. Cardioid Directional Response

Supercardioid/Hypercardioid. The supercardioid and/or hypercardioid microphone picks up sound from a relatively small area on the front part of the capsule (the part of the microphone that captures sound). This pattern gives you the best separation in a live situation. It eliminates all of the sound from the back of the capsule and does a good job of isolating the sound source from the natural ambience of the room and other extraneous sounds. For example, these microphones are particularly good for vocals recorded with limited isolation, a single horn in a section, or a hi-hat. However, use caution when recording with this type of microphone, as the off-axis sounds that are picked up in the front of the microphone can produce a very nasal and crunchy high-frequency effect. (The polar pickup pattern is similar to a cardioid microphone, only more compact.)

Figure-8 or Bidirectional. The figure-8 or bidirectional microphone is common among high-end condensers and older ribbon microphones. The polar pattern (see figure 13.2) shows how the microphone picks up the full range of the sound from both the front and back of the microphone, while eliminating any sound from the sides. The microphone, when configured for a figure-8 pattern, is most useful in two ways. First, when there are two artists performing simultaneously, usually singers, they can face each other. Secondly, when using the M/S (middle/side) microphone setup, you require one microphone to be in the figure-8 configuration. Other than in these situations, you wouldn't typically use this polar pattern.

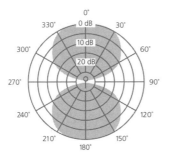

Fig. 13.2. Figure-8 or Bidirectional Response

Omnidirectional. The final pattern, omnidirectional, is one in which the microphone picks up the full range of the sound on a 360° axis around the entire microphone. There are many good uses for this pattern, including group singing, horn sections gathered around the microphone, recording a good room ambience, and so on. This pattern, when used incorrectly, can also record unwelcome, extraneous sounds.

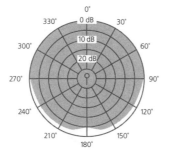

Fig. 13.3. Omnidirectional Response

Study and learn the patterns of the microphones you use. In addition to the frequency response of any particular microphone, the polar pattern provides the quality of the sound you will be recording. Before you buy any microphones, get to know their sound and their common usage. When recording drums, for example, you should never use a condenser or ribbon microphone that is sensitive to loud transients (initial attacks) because the diaphragm could be easily harmed. Conversely, for a gentle sound like an oboe or soft voice, a dynamic microphone that requires a lot of acoustic pressure to move the diaphragm would be insufficient. If you are not familiar with a microphone's distinct characteristics, a knowledgeable sales rep at a pro audio store can point out these differences.

Microphone Overview

Type of Microphone	Directional Response	Cost	Best Application	Common?
Dynamic	Generally cardioid or hypercardioid	$50 and up	Can be used in most applications, but great for drums (snare, toms, and bass drum), guitar, and bass guitar amps	Very common
Condenser	Generally have switchable patterns	$100 and up	Great for sounds that have a lot of overtones and need extreme clarity. For example, vocals, cymbals, acoustic instruments, etc.	Very common
Ribbon	Generally cardioid or hypercardioid, but can be switchable	$1,000 and up	Much the same as condenser microphones, but have a sound coloration and unique clarity	Very rare because of their age and fragile nature
Carbon	Cardioid	$10 and up	Very specific for old-time voice sound or "telephone" sound	Rare because of their age and limited use
Piezo	Omni	$100 and up	Used to capture room sound. Sometimes used for grand piano because of isolation (taped inside lid)	Fairly common, but limited usage
Tube	Switchable patterns	$3,000 and up	Beautiful and warm-sounding microphone for capturing vocals and acoustic instruments	Fairly rare because of price; primarily found in large studios

HEADPHONES, DIRECT BOXES, CABLES, SPLITTER BOXES, VIDEO MONITORS

One of the biggest shocks many first-time recording studio builders encounter is the cost of smaller, "hidden" items—wiring, headphones, splitter boxes, direct boxes, patch cables, and so on. (The cables for my studio cost half as much as the console!) The challenge is to find the best equipment for your budget. There are some must-have items, the first of which is headphones.

HEADPHONES

Even if your studio is just a MIDI/sampling environment and you intend to never record live musicians, it is imperative that you own at least two pairs of studio-quality headphones. Do your shopping at a store that carries pro audio equipment, as opposed to a retail audio store specializing in consumer audio.

The headphones you select should have several features: comfort, isolation from external sound, good sound quality, ability to reproduce music at varying volume levels, and durability. The standard for studio headphones is the AKG K240 Series, which offers all of the above features and is not too expensive. The padded foam earpieces provide acoustic separation from most live instruments. They are light, sound great, and have an impedance that allows large power amps to drive them with ease.

Even if you do use headphones for recording live instruments, you should also have them to monitor mixes. You should *never* mix with headphones, as they are designed with very extreme frequency response and do not give a good representation of what a mix would sound like through a speaker. However, you should *check* your mixes with headphones for any extraneous sounds or lack of stereo balance.

DIRECT BOXES

Another must-have in the recording studio is the direct box. Invented by Geoff Emerick at Abbey Road studios for the Beatles recording sessions, it was initially called the DIT box, or Direct Infusion Transformer box. The direct box is essentially a transformer that converts soft, line-level signals from guitars, bass guitars, synthesizers, and other instruments to microphone levels. This way, the signal is brought in to the console via XLR cables, rather than 1/4-inch cables. This greatly reduces the need to boost the input amplifier on the console to accommodate a low-level signal, and gives a much better frequency response, as well as signal-to-noise ratio. The direct box also eliminates the need for microphone amplifiers that can create a lot of noise in the recording environment, and allows recording to be done in the control room.

Bass guitar and synthesizers are the instruments that engineers most often bring to the console using direct boxes. Recording direct from guitar is less common, though there are products on the market that take the place of the direct box for the guitar and do an excellent job of recreating the natural sound of an amplifier, which is an integral part of guitar recording. For example, on a recent Broadway show I performed in, the entire rhythm section, with the exception of the percussion, used direct inputs to the engineer. The two guitarists used direct boxes or similar equipment that were connected to the console, while the drummer utilized MIDI drum pads to trigger MIDI samples. This avoided acoustic leakage and made the mixing job much easier for the sound designer. All the players then used headphones to monitor their own playing.

Direct boxes come in a variety of configurations and price ranges. There are passive boxes that require no power, boxes that require some kind of battery (usually one 9 volt), and boxes that use phantom power from the console. The latter generally costs the most, but also offers the best quality.

CABLES

Put away quite a few dollars for cables. As everything interfaces with the console, you will need many different types of cables to connect the outboard gear, multitracks, 2-tracks, microphones, direct boxes, power amps, speakers, headphones, and other items to the console. *Don't buy cheap cables.* Cheaper cables lose much of the high-end overtones and tend to break or suffer from poor grounding, creating unnecessary noise.

Some of the various cables you might require include: microphone cables (XLR cables), 1/4-inch guitar cables, 1/4-inch stereo cables, MIDI cables of different lengths, AC extension cables, RCA cables, 1/8-inch stereo cables, speaker cables, TT (Teletype) cables for balanced patch bays, FireWire and optical cables, cables from microphone input panels to microphone inputs on console, input/ output cables for sends and returns to multitrack recorders, and a wide variety of conversion cables (e.g., 1/8-inch stereo mini-plug to stereo pair TT cables). It is often useful to buy a good-quality soldering iron to be able to create or repair cables. This can save a *lot* of money in the long run.

VIDEO MONITOR

Another common item in the writer's studio is the video monitor. If you intend to write music to visuals, this is an important piece of equipment. It can be either a television monitor or computer monitor. Although life is much easier with current sequencing software that synchronizes with video on the computer screen, you really don't get a true feel for the picture until the actual film is being played on a video screen with your music accompanying it. Ideally, get a screen that is at least 25 inches wide, with as high a resolution as possible. If you can afford the latest plasma or LCD flat-screen monitors, your clients will love it.

SPLITTER BOX

Although not always necessary, the splitter box allows several sets of headphones (usually six or eight) to be plugged into it, rather than having many individual cables coming from the headphone output. Each headphone set has its own volume control. The box utilizes one cable from the headphone amplifier and provides the same mix to all of the headphones connected to the box. These are among the easiest studio devices to build yourself, with the parts being readily available at any electronics supply store.

PROJECT 13.1. YOUR GEAR PLAN

List what gear you have, and then list what gear you need. It may help to start backwards from a project. What do you need to make a recording? Consider the processes discussed in this book, and write down only the items that are necessary. Which do you have? How will you research the right product for yourself? What will it cost? Figure out the total cost of your wish list. Then, reconcile this with your budget. Remember, overbuying gear is a common way that writers get into financial difficulty. Come up with a sensible plan, balancing your needs with your budget. Then, have fun building your studio.

CONCLUSION

Outfitting your studio is a never-ending process, and there are always new and better elements to buy. Some items—microphones, computer, software—are critical that you get the best quality you can afford. Other items, such as random effects units, are not as essential.

Let your business needs and your budget guide you, and assemble your studio wisely. It is often a better idea to invest in learning to master your current gear than to purchase a new gadget that you might or might not need.

The Drive to Create Music

THE MULTIFACETED WORK YOU WILL DO AS A WRITER/PRODUCER will keep your days always interesting. There is always something new to learn and do. I hope that you find this aspect of it inspiring.

Unlike how to create a business strategy or how to use a microphone, the last "whiteboard box" I want to share with you is something that I might not be able to teach:

Be Driven!

Maybe, the drive to succeed is the most important feature for making it as a writer/producer. You need to keep at it and be persistent. Find inspiration and let it keep you warm on cold nights. It's the writers who have the most drive that generally succeed.

Here's another story, and I really needed to change the names and details on this one! I had a private student in Toronto who was an extraordinarily hard worker. Call him "Charles." Charles was one of those freakish musicians who did everything really well. He was an excellent drummer. He could play keyboards, guitar, and bass equally well, and was a terrific writer. You just wanted to kill him, except that he was such a nice guy.

We played a gig together one night. Charles was playing keyboards, and I was on bass. A fellow keyboardist came in and said that a well-known rock band was adding a keyboard player, and he was getting the gig.

Charles whispered to me, "I want that gig."

So, Charles found the bandleader's phone number and called. He arranged a meeting. Based on his great demo, they changed their minds and went with Charles, not the other keyboardist.

Charles went touring with the band, playing guitar and keyboards, and sometimes drums, and his name started to get around. Then, a world-class act (you've heard of them) hired him away from the local band, and he began traveling all around the world.

After a year, he'd saved up enough money and made enough connections to follow his real dream: to live in L.A. and produce songs. He's now amazingly wealthy and successful, and living his dream.

Charles was always ready, every time he stepped up to the plate. Charles had the demo, the chops, the personality, and the knowledge. Most of all, he was driven to succeed, and he did really well.

As a writer/producer, your days will be long. You need to have the drive. It can't be a drive to be rich or famous. It must be the drive to be a musician—to do good work, and to make a living writing music. I hope that this book helps you on your journey.

The journey is difficult. By the end of any given semester at Berklee, my students are worn out from all the work that I made them do. You might be feeling the same way, right about now.

Be motivated. Find inspiration in those great musicians and their music that you love. You can be like them, if your heart is there.

So, now what are you going to do?

—Michael Farquharson

Resources

All books published by Berklee Press, except where otherwise noted.

Beall, Eric. *Making Music Make Money*

Davis, Richard. *The Complete Guide to Film Scoring*

Fisher, Jeffrey. *Ruthless Self-Promotion in the Music Industry*. Mix Books, 1999.

Franz, David. *Producing Music with Pro Tools*

———. *Producing Music in the Home Studio*

Hoffert, Paul. *Music for Interactive Media*

Howard, George. *Getting Signed!*

———. *Publishing 101*

Kusek, David and Gerd Leonard. *The Future of Music*

Newhouse, Ben. *Producing Music with Digital Performer*

Spellman, Peter. *The Self-Promoting Musician*

Thompson, Dan. *Understanding Audio*

About the Author

MICHAEL FARQUHARSON has been a writer, producer, engineer, studio owner, and bassist since the early 1970s. His credits include television and radio jingles, films, and many other types of media. As a bassist/ producer/engineer/writer, he has recorded over 150 records. He has also played Broadway shows, and backed up performers ranging from Tom Jones to Brian Auger to Dionne Warwick to Michael Brecker. He has recorded three solo albums (two for the Jazz Inspiration label) and is currently working on a new one with Matthew Nicholl.

Michael has received two Canada Council for the Arts Awards, one Ontario Council for the Arts Award, and several FACTOR (Foundation to Assist Canadian Talent on Records) Awards. His self-titled debut album was nominated for a Juno Award for Best Contemporary Jazz Album. He holds degrees from New England Conservatory and Humber College.

Michael is Professor of Contemporary Writing and Production at Berklee College of Music, where he has taught since 1996. He continues writing/producing commercial music and running his studio, "The Playpen."

Index

Note: Page numbers in *italics* indicate figures.

Serious

about your future in the
music business?

If you're serious about a career in the music industry, you need more than talent. You need to know how to make your music work for you.

Making Music Make Money: An Insider's Guide to Becoming Your Own Music Publisher

ISBN: 0-87639-007-6

An insider's view of the music publishing business, and practical tips toward helping writers effectively assume their rightful role as a publisher of their own music.

BOOK
$26.95

How to Get a Job in the Music and Recording Industry – 2nd Edition

ISBN: 0-87639-072-6

Tips and secrets to educate and empower the serious entertainment industry job seeker.

BOOK
$24.95

Berklee in the Pocket: Music Publishing 101

Get Your Songs Published and Start Earning Royalties!

ISBN: 0-87639-062-9

BOOK
$9.95

Getting Signed! An Insider's Guide to the Record Industry

ISBN: 0-87639-045-9

Arms you with the knowledge you need to work your way through the maze of today's music industry, and move your demo to the top of the stack and get your music heard.

The Self-Promoting Musician

Features tips for writing business olans and press kits, using the Internet for promotion, customized demos, getting music played on college radio, and a comprehensive musician's resource list.

ISBN: 0-634-00644-4

BOOK
$24.95

The Future of Music

Discover the top 10 truths about the music business of the future and how you can benefit from the explosion of digital music.

ISBN: 0-87639-059-9

BOOK
$16.95